*The Path Is the Goal*

D0054831

# The Path Is the Goal

## A BASIC HANDBOOK OF BUDDHIST MEDITATION

### Chögyam Trungpa

Edited by Sherab Chödzin

*Shambhala*
Boston & London
1995

SHAMBHALA PUBLICATIONS, INC.
Horticultural Hall
300 Massachusetts Avenue
Boston, Massachusetts 02115

© 1995 by Diana J. Mukpo

All rights reserved. No part of this book may be
reproduced in any form or by any means, electronic or
mechanical, including photocopying, recording, or by
any information storage and retrieval system, without
permission in writing from the publisher.

9  8  7  6  5  4  3  2  1

FIRST EDITION
Printed in the United States of America on acid-free paper ⊗
Distributed in the United States by Random House, Inc.,
and in Canada by Random House of Canada Ltd

Library of Congress Cataloging-in-Publication Data

Trungpa, Chogyam, 1939–
The path is the goal: a basic handbook of Buddhist meditation / Chögyam
Trungpa ; edited by Sherab Chödzin. — 1st ed.
p.  cm. — (Dharma ocean series)
ISBN 0-87773-970-6
1. Meditation—Buddhism.  I. Chödzin, Sherab.  II. Title.
III. Series: Trungpa, Chogyam, 1939–  Dharma ocean series.
BQ5612.T78  1995                              94-23497
294.3′443—dc20                                    CIP

# Contents

―――

# Editor's Foreword

——

This book comprises two seminars given by the great Tibetan guru, the Vidyadhara, Chögyam Trungpa, Rinpoche, both dating from 1974. The first was given in March in New York, the second in September at Tail of the Tiger, a meditation center the Vidyadhara founded in Vermont, which was later renamed Karmê-Chöling. These seminars contain hitherto unpublished teachings of his on the view and practice of Buddhist meditation.

Traditional accounts tell us that at the time of the Buddha Shakyamuni's enlightenment, he saw a vast panorama of beings throughout the six realms of existence, suffering in their ignorance through an endless round of attachment and disappointment, birth and death. In the literature of the Buddhist tradition we find other accounts of such visions of human suffering. A recent account concerns the Gyalwa Karmapa, Rikpe Dorje (1924–1982), who was the sixteenth incarnation in a line of enlightened hierarchs, heads of the Kagyü order of Buddhism in Tibet. It recounts an incident in his first journey, in the mid-seventies, out of the medieval Himalayan world he had known into the modern West. His first stop was Hong Kong, where his hosts took him to the top of a skyscraper. Standing on the observation platform, the Karmapa looked out with astonishment and delight at the vast view of the city below. Then, after a moment or two, he began to cry. He had to be helped inside by his attendants with tears pouring from his eyes. Later he explained that at the sight of the huge city with its teeming masses being born and struggling and dying without a shred of dharma to help them—"without," as he said, "so much as an OM MANI PADME HUM"—he had been overcome by grief.

From these visions, we do not have to come far to arrive at the job description confronting Trungpa Rinpoche in America. The Vidyadhara was himself the eleventh incarnation in a line of enlightened spiritual and temporal rulers from Eastern Tibet. When he arrived in North America as the sole representative of his lineage in 1970, he saw an exciting and vigorous culture, very full of itself, covering a vast continent. He saw at the same time myriads of individual people suffering through ignorance, through entrenched views about life and lots of aggressive speed. As he himself later described the situation, "Even with . . . encouragement, from the present lineage fathers and my devoted students, I have been left out in the cold as full-time garbageman, janitor, diaper service, and babysitter. So finally I alone have ended up as captain of this great vessel. I alone have to liberate its millions of passengers in this dark age. I alone have to sail this degraded samsaric ocean, which is very turbulent. With the blessings of the lineage, and because of my unyielding vow, there is obviously no choice" (Nālandā Translation Committee/Trungpa, *The Rain of Wisdom* [Boulder, Colo.: Shambhala Publications, 1980], p. xii). In 1970 the eleventh Trungpa Tülku was scarcely thirty. He had been trained intensively in intellectual and meditative disciplines from early childhood, and was regarded by Tibetans as a meditation master of extraordinarily high accomplishment, in full possession of his heritage of awakened mind. Only a few short years in England separated him from the rarefied, protected life of a Tibetan dharma prince. Now he was a penniless immigrant in America. Where to begin?

"The sitting practice of meditation," the Vidyadhara told his listeners, "is the only way." Brilliantly expounding the buddhadharma, he persuaded, cajoled, pleaded, commanded. He rapped the local lingo. He created suitable situations. He did everything he possibly could to get people to apply their bottoms to meditation cushions—except promise results. Only the practice of sitting meditation, as taught by the Buddha himself, could lay the groundwork for an authentic understanding of the Buddha's teaching. If people could sit, and keep sitting, without looking for results, a gap could be created in ego's defenses, and unconditional awareness could begin to shine through.

But ego furiously opposes unconditional awareness.

And its key strategy against meditation's assault, the Vidyadhara taught, is spiritual materialism. This is the attempt to make use of spiritual teachings for our own preconceived purposes. We would like to live longer, be healthier, stronger, more highly competent, more magnetic, more powerful, more highly admired, richer, and more and more invulnerable. What better vehicle toward these ends than profoundest ancient wisdom and techniques of mind training, honed by centuries of application? And if meditation can be tied to ambition, the heart of its power of liberation is gone.

From the beginning the Vidyadhara fought a pitched battle against spiritual materialism. He never tired of explaining in different ways that the true spiritual journey is that of surrender, the gradual abandonment of the reference point of ego through an ever-clearer vision of things as they are. That is why he stunned his audiences over and over by describing, as he does here also, a lonely journey, marked by the painful disappointment of ego's dreams as much as by the joy and freshness of open mind. From the beginning he asked his students to undertake the full rigors of the path as it really is, rather than pitching to their spiritually materialistic appetites. But once they had begun to surrender the reference point of ego, he encouraged, supported, and nurtured their work on themselves in whatever way he could.

The teachings given here on basic meditation—

*shamatha* and *vipashyana,* mindfulness and awareness—provide the foundation that every practitioner needs to awaken as the Buddha did. In addition it was in connection with these basic teachings that the Vidyadhara formulated the overall view of the path of buddhadharma for the first time for Westerners.

I can only hope that readers of this book will be caught by Trungpa Rinpoche's iron hook of compassion. Let us apply ourselves genuinely to the path of meditation.

*Sherab Chödzin*
*Nova Scotia, 1994*

PART ONE

*New York*
*March 1974*

—▲—

# 1

# *The Only Way*

The idea of this particular seminar is to establish a fundamental understanding of the Buddhist approach toward the practice of meditation. Some of you are experienced, some of you are new. In any case, I would like reteach the whole thing. It is very important to develop a basic understanding of meditation, and it is extremely important for you to understand the fundamentals of the Buddhist way of thinking about meditation. This is extremely important for the work that I am doing and we are doing to establish a firm ground of Buddhism in this country. A firm ground would mean people having no misunderstanding whatsoever concerning basic meditation practice and the Buddhist attitude toward enlightenment.

A tradition that developed in Tibet, my country, and other Buddhist countries in medieval times is understanding Buddhism in terms of a three-*yana* process. You begin with the hinayana discipline, then you open yourself to the mahayana level, and then finally you evolve into the vajrayana discipline. So the work we are doing is part of this three-yana approach. I want you to understand the main aspects of this very basic and fundamental process before beginning on the path.

Those who have already begun to tread the path need to reexamine their journey. It is highly important to begin at the beginning rather than starting halfway through without the beginning. That would be like building your castle on an ice block or setting up your apartment in an airplane.

The topic we will be dealing with in this seminar is mindfulness and awareness, which is the basic heart of the Buddhist approach. According to the Buddha, no one can attain basic sanity and basic enlightenment without practicing meditation. You might be highly confused or you might be highly awakened and completely ready for the path. You might be emotionally disturbed and experiencing a sense of claustrophobia in relation to your world. Perhaps you are inspired by works of art you have done or the visual and audial aspects of works of art in general. You might be fat, thin, big, small, intelligent, stupid—whatever you are, there is only one way, unconditionally, and that is to begin with the practice of meditation. The practice of meditation is *the* and *only* way. Without that, there is no way out and no way in.

The practice of meditation is a way of unmasking ourselves, our deceptions of all kinds, and also the practice of meditation is a way of bringing out the subtleties of intelligence that exist within us. The experience of meditation sometimes plays the role of playmate; sometimes it plays the role of devil's advocate, fundamental depression. Sometimes it acts as an encouragement for birth, sometimes as an encouragement for death. Its moods might be entirely different in different levels and states of being and emotion, as well as in the experience of different individuals—but fundamentally, according to the Buddha, Shakyamuni Buddha, there is no doubt, none whatsoever, that meditation is the only way for us to begin on the spiritual path. That is the only way. *The* way.

Meditation is a way of realizing the fundamental truth, the basic truth, that we can discover ourselves, we can work on ourselves. The goal is the path and the path is the goal. There is no other way of attaining basic sanity than the practice of meditation. Absolutely none. The evidence for that is that for two thousand five hundred years since the time of the Buddha, down through the lineage of enlightened teachers from generation to generation, people have gained liberation through the practice of meditation. This is not a myth. It's reality. It actually did exist, it does exist; it did work, it did happen, it does work, it does happen. But without the practice of meditation, there is no way.

Let us discuss the term *meditation* at this point. When we talk about the practice of meditation, we are talking about a way of being. Unfortunately, the term *meditation* is not quite an adequate translation of the Sanskrit term *dhyana* or *samadhi*. Whenever we use a verbal form like "to meditate" or "meditating," that automatically invites the question, "What are you meditating upon?" or "What are you meditating in?" That is a common question that always comes up. But according to the Buddha's philosophy, there is no verb "to meditate." There is just a noun, "meditation." There's no meditat*ing*. You don't meditate, but you be in a state of meditation. You might find it very hard to swallow this distinction. We have a linguistic, a grammatical problem here. Meditating is not part of the Buddhist vocabulary, but meditation is.

"Meditation" is a noun that denotes that you are being in a state of meditation *already*. Whereas "meditat*ing*" gives the idea of an activity that's taking place all the time, that you're meditating on this or that, concentrating on flickering candlelight, watching an incense stick burning, listening to your pulse, your heartbeat, listening to the inner tunes of your mantric utterance going on in your head—whatever. But according to the buddhadharma, meditation is a simple factor. You don't meditate, you just be in the meditation. *Dhyana* is a noun rather than a verb. It refers to being in a state of dhyana, rather than "dhyana-ing." Meditation in this case has no object, no purpose, no reference point. It is simply individuals willing to take a discipline on themselves, not to please God or the

Buddha or their teacher or themselves. Rather one just sits, one holds oneself together. One sits a certain length of time. One just simply sits without aim, object, purpose, without anything at all. Nothing whatsoever. One just *sits.*

You might ask, "Then what does one do if one sits? Shouldn't one be doing something? Or is one just sitting there hanging out?" Well, there's a difference between sitting and "hanging out" in the American idiom. The term *hanging out* means something like "grooving on your scene." And sitting is just being there like a piece of rock or a disused coffee cup sitting on the table. So meditation is not regarded as hanging out but just sitting and being, simply.

Questions often come up like, "Why the hell am I doing this, behaving like an idiot, just sitting?" And people also experience a lot of resentment. They think: "I've been told to sit like this. Somebody's making fun of me, taking advantage of my gullibility. Somebody has made me just sit like that, just sit. I'm not even allowed to hang out. I have to just sit on my meditation cushion." But the instruction to do that is actually an extremely important, powerful message. If we learn to sit properly, thoroughly, and fully, that is the best thing we could do at this point.

If we look back on the history of our life since we were born, since we first went to school, we never sat. We never sat. We might have hung out occasionally and experienced utter boredom and felt sorry for ourselves. Feeling bored and preoccupied, we might have hung out occasionally on street corners or in our living rooms watching television, chewing our chewing gum, and so forth. But we never sat. We never sat like a rock. We never did. How about that?

Here, this is the first experience in our life of sitting—not hanging out or perching—but actually sitting on the ground on a meditation cushion. Just that to begin with, to say nothing for the moment about techniques for how you sit. Before we discuss techniques, let us point out the merit—*punya* in Sanskrit—the very merit and sanity and wakefulness you are going to get out of this, out of just simply being willing to sit like a piece of rock. It's fantastically powerful. It overrides the atom bomb. It's extraordinarily powerful that we decide just to sit, not hang out or perch, but just sit on a meditation cushion. Such a brave attitude, such a wonderful commitment is magnificent. It is very sane, extraordinarily sane.

We usually don't sit on the ground. We sit on chairs. The closest we get to just sitting is when we sit still for ten or twenty hours as passengers or drivers in our cars. But then we are entertained by the road, by the traveling, by the speed. We think we are sitting, but still we are getting somewhere. We are still traveling. Apart from that, we have never known actually sitting on the ground properly and thoroughly and fully like a rock, like a sitting buddha. We have never done that. That is an extraordinary experience. This is an important point. This is what we actually miss in this world. When we sit, it is always for a purpose. If we are sitting in a car, we are thinking, "How long is it going to take me to get to my destination, so I can begin to rush?" We count mileage, note the speed of our car, watch the speedometer. We sit for a purpose. It is a very interesting point that nobody has experienced that we can actually sit on a cushion without any purpose, none whatsoever. It is outrageous. Nobody would actually ever do that. We can't even think about it. It's unthinkable. It's terrible—we would be wasting our time.

Now there's the point—wasting our time. Maybe that's a good one, wasting our time. Give time a rest. Let it be wasted. Create virgin time, uncontaminated time, time that hasn't been hassled by aggression, passion, and speed. Let us create pure time. Sit and create pure time.

That is a very important thing. It might sound crazy to you, impractical, but it is very important to think in those terms. Sitting practice is a revolutionary idea for Westerners, but not as far as Buddhists are concerned. Buddha did it. Buddha did it two thousand five hundred years ago. He sat and wasted his time. And he transmitted the knowledge to us that it is the best thing we can do for ourselves—waste our time by sitting. The very idea of aggression and passion could be tamed by sitting practice. Just sitting like a piece of rock is a very important point.

We can discuss the techniques later, but right now I don't want to overcrowd your mind. I want you to think about the importance of wasting time sitting, slowing down, becoming like a piece of rock. It's the first message of the Buddha.

My particular lineage is the Kagyü lineage. *Kagyü* means "follower of the sacred word." And this lineage is also known as the *drubgyü,* "the practicing lineage." We have been known for this emphasis on practice. We understand that the emphasis on practice is very important. And my lineage has produced millions of sane people in the past. And is doing so in the present as well. We have evidence of that.

Sitting practice is the basic point, before we embark on any spiritual disciplines at all, especially in Buddhism. The teachings of Buddha are presented in a threefold way, as we mentioned. And on the hinayana level alone, we have *shila, samadhi,* and *prajna*—discipline, meditation, and intellect. And before we begin with shila—discipline—of any kind, we have to learn to slow down. That is the basic discipline of how to be. So the basic way to learn to behave in a buddha-like way is sitting practice. Then, after that, we develop meditation, samadhi, and knowledge, prajna. Before we learn to spell words, we have to learn our ABCs. We have to be actually willing to accept the boredom of sitting, willing to relate with that particular sanity, which is unconditional sanity. This sanity has nothing to do with fighting against insanity or trying to exorcise it. It is just fundamentally, basically, trying to be simple as what we are. That is the basic point according to Buddha.

STUDENT: Rinpoche, could you say something about merit?

TRUNGPA RINPOCHE: Merit is a sense of richness and a sense of reward, which can only develop by not creating further complications in our confusion. Just sitting and doing nothing is the best way of all to produce merit.

STUDENT: Could you say something about the difference between the complexity, the complicated structure, of neurosis and what maybe could be called the simple richness of sanity?

TRUNGPA RINPOCHE: Complexity is also very simple. It is so complex it becomes simple. I don't see any problems with that, particularly. You look up at the sky and see the stars, thousands of millions of them. They seem to be very complicated. It's difficult to name them, find out what they are, and so on. But still, it's the simple sky. The complexity and the simplicity amount to the same thing. Confusion and complexity are the expression of simplicity.

STUDENT: Discipline in sitting practice seems very comforting to me. It tells me what to do. Then I get up from my sitting practice and I light a cigarette. I would like a rule of discipline that tells me I should not light the cigarette as I'm told I should sit. I'm always in confusion about where rules are given or where a suggestion for discipline is given and where they're withheld or not presented.

TRUNGPA RINPOCHE: These rules and regulations are not homemade recipes. The rules and regulations that have developed in the Buddhist tradition are extremely official and efficient and very powerful. Those rules and regulations are no longer a domestic matter connected with your comfort. The rules and regulations are fundamental openness. If you feel there's something wrong about lighting a cigarette, don't regard it as your problem. Or for that matter, don't regard having sexual fantasies in the middle of your sitting practice or having aggression fantasies—how you're going to punch your enemy in the nose—as your problems. All kinds of things like that happen, but they are no longer regarded as problems. They are regarded as a promise, in fact. Those are the only working basis that we have. Those are the only working basis that we have in our practice of meditation. Without those, we are completely sterile, cleaned out with Ajax, like hospital corridors where there's no place for germs. The path of dharma, the *dharma marga,* provides all kinds of problems, obstacles, and we work along with those. Without that path, we would fall asleep. Suppose highways were without any bends, just like Roman roads, a one-shot deal straight from New York to Washington, 100 percent straight. The drivers would fall asleep. Because of that, there would be more accidents than if the road had bends in it with road signs here and there. The path is personal experience, and one should take delight in those little things that go on in our lives, the obstacles, seductions, paranoias, depressions, and openness. All kinds of things happen, and that is the content of the journey, which is extremely powerful and important. Without those problems, we cannot tread on the path. We should feel grateful that we are in the samsaric world, so that we can tread the path, that we are not sterile, completely cleaned out, that the world has not been taken over by some computerized system. There's still room for rawness and ruggedness and roughness all over the place. Good luck!

# 2

# *Continuing Your Confusion*

⎯⎯

Having laid the basic groundwork regarding the practice of meditation, we can now go further and discuss the point that the practice of meditation involves a basic sense of continuity. The practice of meditation does not involve discontinuing one's relationship with oneself and looking for a better person or searching for possibilities of reforming oneself and becoming a better person. The practice of meditation is a way of continuing one's confusion, chaos, aggression, and passion— but working with it, seeing it from the enlightened point of view. That is the basic purpose of meditation practice as far as this approach is concerned.

There is a Sanskrit term for basic meditation practice, *shamatha,* which means "development of peace." In this case, peace refers to the harmony connected with accuracy rather than to peace from the point of view of pleasure rather than pain. We have experienced pain, discomfort, because we have failed to relate with the harmony of things as they are. We haven't seen things as they are precisely, directly, properly, and because of that we have experienced pain, chaotic pain. But in this case when we talk about peace we mean that for the first time we are able to see ourselves completely, perfectly, beautifully *as what we are,* absolutely as what we are.

This is more than raising the level of our potentiality. If we talk in those terms, it means we are thinking of an embryonic situation that will develop: this child may be highly disturbed, but he has enormous potentiality of becoming a reasonable, less disturbed personality. We have a problem with language here, an enormous problem. Our language is highly involved with the realm of possessions and achievements. Therefore, we have a problem in expressing with this language the notion of unconditional potentiality, which is the notion that is applicable here.

Shamatha meditation practice is the vanguard practice for developing our mindfulness. I would like to call your attention to this term, *mindfulness.* Generally, when we talk about mindfulness, it has to do with a warning sign, like the label on your cigarette package where the surgeon general tells you this is dangerous to your health—beware of this, be mindful of this. But here mindfulness is not connected with a warning. In fact, it is regarded as more of a welcoming gesture: you could be fully minded, mindful. Mindfulness means that you could be a wholesome person, a completely wholesome person, rather than that you should not be doing this or that. Mindfulness here does not mean that you should look this way or that way so you can be cured of your infamous problems, whatever they are, your problems of being mindless. Maybe you think like this: you are a highly distracted person, you have problems with your attention span. You can't sit still for five minutes or even one minute, and you should control yourself. Everybody who practices meditation begins as a naughty boy or naughty girl who has to learn to control himself or herself. They should learn to pay attention to their desk, their notebook, their teacher's blackboard.

That is the attitude that is usually connected with the idea of mindfulness. But the approach here has nothing to do with going back to school, and mindfulness has nothing to do with your attention span as you experienced it in school at all. This is an entirely new angle, a new approach, a development of peace, harmony, openness.

The practice of meditation, in the form of shamatha at the beginner's level, is simply being. It is bare attention that has nothing to do with a warning. It is just simply being and keeping a watchful eye, completely and properly. There are traditional disciplines, techniques, for that, mindfulness techniques. But it is very difficult actually to explain the nature of mindfulness. When you begin trying to develop mindfulness in the ordinary sense, a novice sense, your first flash of thought is that you are unable to do such a thing. You feel that you may not be able to accomplish what you want to do. You feel threatened. At the same time, you feel very romantic: "I am getting into this new discipline, which is a unique and very powerful thing for me to do. I feel joyous, contemplative, monkish (or 'nunkish'). I feel a sense of renunciation, which is very romantic."

Then the actual practice begins. The instructors tell you how to handle your mind and your body and your awareness and so on. In practicing shamatha under those circumstances, you feel like a heavily loaded pack donkey trying to struggle across a highly polished stream of ice. You can't grip it with your hooves, and you have a heavy load on your back. At the same time, people are hitting you from behind, and you feel so inadequate and so embarrassed. Every beginning meditator feels like an adolescent donkey, heavily loaded and not knowing how to deal with the slippery ice. Even when you are introduced to various mindfulness techniques that are supposed to help you, you still feel the same thing—that you are dealing with a foreign element, which you are unable to deal with properly. But you feel that you should at least show your faith and bravery, show that you are willing to go through the ordeal of the training, the challenge of the discipline.

The problem here is not so much that you are uncertain how to practice meditation, but that you haven't identified the teachings as personal experience. The teachings are still regarded as a foreign element coming into your system. You feel you have to do your best with that sense of foreignness, which makes you a clumsy young donkey. The young donkey is being hassled by his master a great deal, and he is already used to carrying a heavy load and to being hit every time there is a hesitation. In that picture the master becomes an external entity rather than the donkey's own conviction. A lot of the problems that come up in the practice of meditation have to do with a fear of foreignness, a sense that you are unable to relate with the teachings as part of your basic being. That becomes an enormous problem.

The practice of shamatha meditation is one of the most basic practices for becoming a good Buddhist, a well-trained person. Without that, you cannot take even a step toward a personal understanding of the true buddhadharma. And the buddhadharma, at this point, is no myth. We know that this practice and technique was devised by the Buddha himself. We know that he went through the same experiential process. Therefore, we can follow his example.

The basic technique here is identification with one's breath or, when doing walking meditation, identification with one's walking. There is a traditional story that Buddha told an accomplished musician that he should relate to controlling his mind by keeping it not too tight and not too loose. He should keep his mind at the right level of attention. So, as we practice these techniques, we should put 25 percent of our attention on the breathing or the walking. The rest of our mental activities should be let loose, left open. This has nothing to do with the vajrayana or crazy wisdom or anything like that at all. It is just practical advice. When you tell somebody to keep a high level of concentration, to concentrate 100 percent and not make any mistakes, that person becomes stupid and is liable to make more mistakes because he's so concentrated on what he's doing. There's no gap. There's no room to open himself, no room to relate with the back-and-forth play between the reference point of the object and the reference point of the subject. So the Buddha quite wisely advised that you put only tentative attention on your technique, not to make a big deal out of concentrating on the technique (this method is mentioned in the *Samadhiraja-sutra*). Concentrating too heavily on the technique brings all kinds of mental activities, frustrations, and sexual and aggressive fantasies of all kinds. So you keep just on the verge of your technique, with just 25 percent of your attention. Another 25 percent is relaxing, a further 25 percent relates to making friends with oneself, and the last 25 percent connects with expectation—your mind is open to the possibility of something happening during this practice session. The whole thing is synchronized completely.

These four aspects of mindfulness have been referred to in the *Samadhiraja-sutra* as the four wheels of a chariot. If you have only three wheels, there's going to be a strain on the chariot as well as the horse. If you have two, the chariot will be heavy to the point of not being functional—the horse will have to hold up the whole thing and pull as well. If, on the other hand, you had five or six wheels on your chariot, that would create a bumpy ride and the passengers would not feel all that comfortable. So the ideal number of wheels we should have on our chariot is four, the four techniques of meditation: concentration, openness, awareness, expectation. That leaves a lot of room for play. That is the approach of the buddhadharma, and we know that a lot of people in the lineage have practiced that way and have actually achieved a perfect state of enlightenment in one lifetime.

The reason why the technique is very simple is that, that way, we cannot elaborate on our spiritual-materialism trip.[1] Everyone breathes, unless they are dead. Everyone walks, unless they are in a wheelchair. And those techniques are the simplest and the most powerful, the most immediate, practical, and relevant to our life. In the case of breathing, there is a particular tradition that has developed from a commentary on the *Samadhiraja-sutra* written by Gampopa. There we find the notion, related to breathing, of mixing mind and space, which is also used in tantric meditative practices. But even at the hinayana level, there is a mixing of mind and space. This has become one of the very important techniques of meditation. Sometimes this particular approach is also referred to as *shi-lhak sung juk,* which is a Tibetan expression meaning "combining shamatha and vipashyana meditation practices."

Combining shamatha and vipashyana plays an important part in the meditator's development. Mindfulness becomes awareness. Mindfulness is taking an interest in precision of all kinds, in the simplicity of the breath, of walking, of the sensations of the body, of the experiences of the mind—of the thought process and memories of all kinds. Awareness is acknowledging the totality of the whole thing. In the Buddhist tradition, awareness has been described as the first experience of egolessness. The term for awareness in Tibetan is *lhak-thong,*[2] and there is an expression *lhakthong dagme tokpe sherap,* which means "the knowledge that realizes egolessness through awareness." This is the first introduction to the understanding of egolessness. Awareness in this case is totality rather than one-sidedness. A person who has achieved awareness or who is working on the discipline of awareness has no direction, no bias in one direction or another. He is just simply aware, totally and completely. This awareness also includes precision, which is the main quality of awareness in the early stage of the practice of meditation.

Awareness brings egolessness because there is no object of awareness. You are aware of the whole thing completely, of you and other and of the activities of you and other at the same time. So everything is open. There is no particular object of the awareness.

If you're smart enough, you might ask the question, "Who is being aware of this whole thing?" That's a very interesting question, the sixty-four-dollar question. And the answer is, nobody is being aware of anything but *itself*. The razor blade cuts itself. The sun shines by itself. Fire burns by itself. Water flows by itself. Nobody watches—and that is the very primitive logic of egolessness.

I'm sure the mahayanists would sneer and think that this is terrible logic, very crude. They probably would not hold high opinions of it. But from the point of view of hinayana, that's extraordinarily fantastic logic. Razor blade cuts itself; fire burns itself; water quenches thirst by itself.[3] This is the egolessness of vipashyana practice.

Traditionally, we have the term *smriti-upasthana* in Sanskrit, or *satipatthana* in Pali, which means resting in one's intelligence. This is the same as awareness. Awareness here does not mean that the person practicing vipashyana meditation gives up his or her shamatha techniques of, say, *anapanasati*—mindfulness of the coming and going of the breath—or of walking in walking meditation practice. The meditator simply relates with that discipline in a more expansive way. He or she begins to relate with the whole thing. This is done in connection with what is known as the four foundations of mindfulness: mindfulness of body, of mind, of livelihood, and of effort.[4]

If you relate with every move you make in your sitting practice of meditation, if you take note of every detail, every aspect of the movement of your mind, of the relationships in everything that you do, there's no room for anything else at all. Every area is taken over by meditation, by vipashyana practice. So there is no one to practice and nothing to practice. No you actually exists. Even if you think, "I am practicing this particular technique," you really have no one there to relate to, no one to talk to. Even at the moment when you say, "I am practicing," that too is an expression of awareness at the same time, so you have nothing left, nothing whatsoever, even no "I am practicing." You can still say the empty words, but they are like a lion's corpse, as it has been traditionally described. When the lion is dead, the lion's corpse remains lying in the jungle, and the other animals continue to be frightened of the lion. The only ones who can destroy the lion's corpse are the worms who crawl up from underneath and do not see it from the outside. They eat through it, so finally the lion's corpse disintegrates on the ground. So the worms are like the awareness, the

knowledge that realizes egolessness through awareness—vipashyana.

STUDENT: You characterized shamatha as mindfulness
and vipashyana as awareness. Then you went on to
speak of the combination of shamatha and vipashyana.
How would you characterize that?

TRUNGPA RINPOCHE: It's a combination of the two,
of being precise and at the same time being open. Precision is shamatha and openness is vipashyana, and it is
possible to have both of those happening together.

S: But don't they already happen together in vipashyana? Isn't the development of vipashyana based on the
precision of shamatha, which vipashyana then goes on
to include in its openness or awareness?

TR: That is precisely why we talk about shamatha-
vipashyana. One of the interesting points is that even
at the level of *maha ati* or the *mahamudra* experience—on the tantric level of awarenesss—shamatha
and vipashyana still function. They still are valid, because you have developed this basic way of taming your
mind, and it is still developing.

S: But if vipashyana includes or is based on shamatha,
why do we have to bother to speak of shamatha-
vipashyana?

TR: Further clarity and further precision develop. Shamatha comes back again at the level of the sixth *bhumi*
of the bodhisattva path, when the bodhisattva has

achieved the *paramita* of *prajna*. He still comes back to shamatha, and vipashyana comes back again as well. There is a second round.

S: Maybe it's that vipashyana is a stance of openness, and as such, maybe it's a little too loose.

TR: That's right. It loses its perspective, so there is a constant renewal of things happening. Then the same thing happens again on the tantric level of *kriya* yoga, which is the first of the six yanas of tantra, involved with purity. You begin your precision once more. Then it happens again at the level of the yanas of the higher tantra, *mahayoga* yana, the first of the *ati* yanas. There again, you bring back your precision of relating with certain mandalas and the experience of phenomena. So there's a constant recalling, again and again throughout the nine yanas. The precision of shamatha practice is always recalled, again and again.

STUDENT: Rinpoche, could you clarify satipatthana a little bit?

TRUNGPA RINPOCHE: Satipatthana, or smriti-upasthana, as it is known in Sanskrit, is the basic mindfulness practice that goes on in both shamatha and vipashyana. It is made up of the four foundations of mindfulness, *drenpa nyewar shakpa shi* in Tibetan, which means resting your cognitive mind, mindfulness. That is always a very important point. Without that, it is impossible to begin on the Buddhist path at all. It is the foundation of your building. Without going through that process, you have misunderstandings of vajrayana, misunderstandings of mahayana, and of course misunderstandings of hinayana. So satipatthana is the only way that is taught. It is a very important basic beginning. A person cannot begin any spiritual discipline without that, because his mind will not be tamed. Basic sanity will not be developed. No reconciliation, or acceptance, will have developed at the beginner's level.

S: It's not easy.

TR: It's very hard, very difficult. That's why we call the beginning level hinayana, the narrow path, which is very severe, extremely severe. It's not a matter of being happy and having fun, particularly. It's verrrry difficult.

S: It has to be conquered.

TR: Has to be reconciled, or rather, you have to become reconciled to it. That's why there are going to be very rare Buddhists who are actually going to involve themselves with such a process. They will be what is known as golden Buddhists, who have been burned and hammered and have finally turned into pure gold, beyond the twenty-four-carat level, very fine gold. This is very difficult, but it is better to have golden Buddhists than copper Buddhists.

STUDENT: Rinpoche, in meditation practice, when you're beginning to develop vipashyana and you become aware of the space around the breath, is there is no longer a watcher involved?

TRUNGPA RINPOCHE: There is still a watcher involved, but the watcher is no longer regarded as problematic. The watcher is regarded as a vehicle.

S: So should one encourage the watcher during meditation?

TR: One doesn't do anything with the watcher. One just lives with the watcher.

S: How is the watcher a vehicle?

TR: Well, we don't have anything else but the watcher for a vehicle. At that point, the only intelligent voice that you have is the watcher. For lack of a better choice, that's it. Sometimes the watcher is referred to as self-consciousness. In the Christian tradition, it might be referred to as a guilt conflict—whatever.

STUDENT: If you put 25 percent concentration on the breath and 25 percent on relaxation, and so on— the way you described—does that create a problem with identifying with the breath as you have taught us to do?

TRUNGPA RINPOCHE: Absolutely not. It provides more possibility of identifying. Take a very simple example. People find it very conducive when they're watching movies to eat popcorn. Twenty-five percent, maybe 50 percent of their attention is on the screen and another 25 percent is on popcorn, and another 25 percent is on their companion or their Coca-Cola, or whatever. Which makes the whole experience of going to the cinema very pleasurable. That's precisely the whole point. You develop enormous concentration. You follow the dialogue in the movie and you follow every detail of the story, and you have a good time at the movies.

STUDENT: It seems to me that once you gave some instruction before we were going to meditate like, "Don't be the watcher."

TRUNGPA RINPOCHE: You can't be the watcher anyway, but if you try to be the watcher, that just creates further problems. It's like leprosy: once you have one sore, that expands and develops another, and another sore is constantly developing. So the less watcher, the more clean-cut. But rather than trying to abandon the watcher, you just don't take part in the watcher's trip.

S: Is the watcher your reference point?

TR: Reference point *is* the watcher. The reference point referring to itself is the watcher. There is no other watcher other than the reference point. That's the whole point—that all kinds of reference points become the watcher.

STUDENT: When I'm meditating I see words, and some of them seem to be other people's thoughts and some of them seem to be communications from somewhere else, and some of them seem to be directions. And it's very hard to really distinguish what's what.

TRUNGPA RINPOCHE: Why bother?

S: Just to clarify.

TR: Why bother?

S: I suppose I can just try to ride through the confusion, but—

TR: There's no point trying to sort out whose confusion is whose. That would be like trying to sort out whose dollar is whose, and every nickel and every cent. The whole thing becomes very complicated. Maybe some analytical disciplines might encourage you to sort out the problem of the universe bit by bit, but we Buddhists are very sloppy, I'm afraid. We don't bother to count our pennies. We just deal with dollars, or twenty-dollar checks, or seven-hundred-dollar checks. It's just simply money. It doesn't matter who each cent came from. That doesn't seem to present any problems.

S: I'm a writer. I try to record it.

TR: Well, you have to write very simply. The possibilities are, you might become a more successful writer if you simplify the plot. Make it very clean-cut, which is very intriguing at the same time, maybe very mysterious. That makes a best-seller.

S: I don't know. I wouldn't really know how to simplify.

TR: Don't try to. That's the starting point.

STUDENT: Making friends with yourself.

TRUNGPA RINPOCHE: Well said.

STUDENT: Can you make a distinction between hope and expectation, which is one of the things that you listed for 25 percent attention? You once said it was necessary to give up hope, and I really don't see too much distinction there.

TRUNGPA RINPOCHE: Hope is future-oriented. Expectation is much closer to reality, but still not quite getting to the reality. It's on the verge of reality. Hope is like saying, "I hope I could be the mother of a child." Expectation means you are already pregnant, that it is already happening in real life, that you are going to bear a child. Which is much more immediate.

STUDENT: What is perfect enlightenment, which you mentioned in your talk?

TRUNGPA RINPOCHE: The Sanskrit term is *samyak-sambuddha,* which traditionally means enlightenment without any reference point. So there is no certainty whether you have actually attained enlightenment or not. You *are.* If you look at it from our angle, it might be very dull, disappointing. But once you are there, you find it is completely spacious. The whole thing doesn't sound that glamorous, eh?

STUDENT: How do you avoid creating a better speedy confused situation by doling out your awareness into concentration and expectation, et cetera? It seems to me that in meditation practice, just as in the rest of your life, you try to keep on top of what you're doing and create space at the same time. And it only creates more confusion.

TRUNGPA RINPOCHE: I think the only thing to do is try not to sort out what is better and what is not better. Sorting out produces further problems. Gesundheit.

STUDENT: Is there a point in meditation practice where you practice letting go of the watcher or reference point, or is it something that just falls away by itself?

TRUNGPA RINPOCHE: There's no telling. No promise.

S: Is letting go of the reference point something you consciously practice?

TR: No promise. *Duhkha,* suffering, is regarded as the first noble truth. Discovering duhkha is also regarded as one of the noble truths. And the path is regarded as a noble truth and the goal is regarded as a noble truth. All the four noble truths are equally valid in themselves. One can't say which one is the best truth. All four are noble truths. Good luck!

S: I don't understand at all.

TR: Well, think about it. You can't sort out which is the best one.

S: The question I think I was asking was related to the practice itself: whether letting go is something active or something that just happens through the practice of watching the breath.

TR: Both are saying the same thing. Letting go is watching the breath, watching the breath is letting go. Saying the same thing.

STUDENT: Could meditation and these techniques you've been talking about be regarded as a form of psychotherapy?

TRUNGPA RINPOCHE: Psychotherapy is analyzing oneself and providing medication—being therapeutic. But meditation is not regarded as medicine or even as therapeutic. It is just an unconditional way of being in life.

S: Well, is it parallel at all to existential therapy in philosophy and practice?

TR: Somewhat, but the Buddhist approach is more boring. There's no glamour involved.

STUDENT: I've been wondering what dangers one can encounter in meditation, if there are dangers that exist.

TRUNGPA RINPOCHE: If one becomes involved in contemplative practices which entail contemplating all kinds of visual objects without first having developed basic shamatha and vipashyana, it could be quite dangerous. The scriptures say that if you become involved in visualizing without basic training of the mind, you could become Rudra, an egomaniac. Apart from that, if a person is following a very simple technique of medi-

tation practice and has a background in the basic training, there's no problem at all. That is why shamatha,
for example, is called "development of peace." It is
harmless, very kind. That's why vipashyana is called
development of insight or awareness—because it sharp-
ens your basic being. It is designed for those people
who are following the first stages of the path.

According to the Buddhist tradition, there are five
paths that make up the path: the path of accumulation,
the path of unification, the path of seeing, the path of
meditation, and the path of no more learning. So in
this case, being a beginner, you are starting on the path
of accumulation. Traditionally, a person on the path
of accumulation should begin with shamatha practice,
which is a harmless practice, but at the same time very
fruitful. That's how the Buddha designed the path.
And it seems it has been working for two thousand five
hundred years. Nobody has gone utterly crazy except
those people who didn't follow his path.

STUDENT: How do you reconcile what you said in your
first talk about being willing to waste time and what
you talked about tonight about 25 percent expectation? I mean, a rock doesn't expect anything. It's just
sitting there. That's what you said in your first talk.
Then tonight, we're expecting something.

TRUNGPA RINPOCHE: That's also wasting time. Expecting something is wasting your time as well, because you are not going to get anything.

S: So wasting time is not part of your feeling, then. You don't feel like you're wasting time.

TR: It doesn't really matter what you do, you're still wasting time. You don't have to make a martyr of yourself, saying, "I feel great because I'm wasting my time. I'm being a perfectly good Buddhist and a good meditator, because I'm wasting my time."

S: So wasting time with that attitude . . . that really isn't an attitude that you want to cultivate.

TR: Wasting time's not an attitude. It's just a fact.

# 3

# *The Star of Bethlehem*

To understand the relationship of awareness and being, we have to look into the notion of being at this point. There are all kinds of approaches toward being. Being good, being bad, being sensible, being crazy. Beatitude [be-attitude]. All kinds of notions of being. But when we talk about being in relation to awareness, we are talking about unconditional being. You just be. Without any questions about *what* you are being. It is an unconditional way of being.

Unconditional being is a state of mind which is involved with a certain attitude. You might say: "Could that be unconditional mind if it is involved with an attitude? If it is also an attitude, we couldn't define it as unconditional being." True. But oddly enough, even unconditional being requires an attitude in order to develop to the unconditional level. We have to make some condition in order to develop unconditionality. We cannot begin perfectly. Otherwise it would cease being the beginning and become the end, an achievement.

The reason we refer to this whole process as the beginner's level is that it is the level of clumsiness, the level of messiness. It is unstructured, confused, and so forth. There is confusion, messiness, untidiness—and constant dichotomy, constant reference point. But at least we are moving in the direction of unconditional being.

We are gazing at the star of Bethlehem on the horizon. It is far, far away, but still there is hope. A spark of luminosity is there. The land may be dark, the sky may be gray and black. It might be chilly, and we might be cold, uncomfortable, tired, and restless. But nevertheless, the star of Bethlehem is over there. Human beings hope. The final hope that human beings could ever be hopeful of is enlightenment, the star of Bethlehem on the horizon.

The buddhas, *tathagatas,* and great teachers have developed skillful means throughout the ages. Their approach is to hold up enlightenment like a carrot in front of a donkey. There is a carrot thousands of miles away shining, and you have to walk and walk and walk and go get it. The donkey doesn't have the carrot at this point, at the beginner's level, but he has to be inspired. So a faraway inspiration is provided. Something is taking place way off there on the horizon. There is a big space, a huge desert landscape.

The point (apart from all this poetic imagery) is that we need hope, the powerful hope of attaining enlightenment in this lifetime. We need that hope because of having to relate with the constant chatter that goes on in our mind, the emotional ups and downs of all kinds that go on, the disturbances that we experience, the constant, ongoing process taking place in our state of being. We need a reference point connected with that.

Hope can be categorized into two types. Spiritual aspiration is one, and the hope of gaining power is another. As far as aspiration is concerned, the students need to relate with a spiritual friend, a *kalyanamitra* in Sanskrit, *gewe she-nyen* in Tibetan. A spiritual friend is very important. You cannot start even at the beginning of the beginning without relating with a person who has gone through this particular journey and achieved results, enlightenment. It is necessary to have that kind of reference point, a lineage holder, a craftsman. You have to have information. You have to gather information about the handicraft—how the knowledge is passed down. You have to relate with somebody who knows how to make the dharma part of a visible world rather than letting it remain a myth. The spiritual friend, kalyanamitra, is a person who avoids a speculative attitude toward the teaching. He keeps it from being mythical. He brings it about in reality. He has done it, you can do it. It is possible and visible. It is obvious.

Such a relationship could begin purely through the fame of a certain spiritual friend, or guru for that matter, a person who is reputed to have power over other people's confusion. Confusion doesn't exist when you meet a certain guru. You could follow such a person by faith, or else you could have a personal experience. You could experience that meeting such a person is very powerful. You could actually experience that in the presence of such a person, you experience your own basic sanity, a sense of solidness. A sense of reality actually takes place.

So there are two choices. Either you could be the blind-faith type, who just believes and worships without logic. Or else you could be the type of person who doesn't believe, who is extremely skeptical, highly opinionated, full of his own philosophies of all kinds. A person like that could still meet a spiritual friend on an eye-level basis and could explore how he is, why he is, and what level of spiritual operation he is performing. That doesn't mean to suggest that to pass your examination the spiritual friend has to be levitating three inches above you or constantly emanating sparks of enlightenment in the form of fireworks. It is the personal relationship that is very important.

Traditionally the guru is described as like the sun shining on the earth. Every aspect of this earth—every flower petal, every leaf, every blade of grass that grows—is related to the sun in accordance with the four seasons. Each flower on this earth has a personal relationship with the sun, although the sun does not particularly personally direct its attention with any bias, does not actually shine more on the rosebush than on the poppy or anything like that. The whole process depends on how much receptivity there is, how much openness.

So personal openness is the important thing, rather than purely living on faith. Faith can be blind or intelligent. Open faith is intelligent, being willing to include one's confusion and one's understanding at the same time. Blind faith is purely going by facts and figures, thinking in terms of quick results, depending on fame, reputation, and so forth. It is like saying you should read this book because this book is a best-seller. Five million copies have been sold, therefore it must be good. It is possible that five million stupid people bought it and read it. But that's the kind of reference point followed by blind faith.

So in following the spiritual path it is very much necessary to have a personal relationship with a teacher, a kalyanamitra, a *gewe she-nyen.* The spiritual teacher presents you with the star of Bethlehem. He takes you out of your cozy home. Maybe outside it is brisk or even biting cold. He says: "Shall we put our coat on? Let's just step out and take a look at what's happening in the universe."

So it is a cold winter night and your spiritual friend decides to take you out on a walk. He says, "Put on your boots. Don't punish yourself. Wear a coat, a warm coat. If you like, take a cigar along with you. Now let us take a walk, step out of our mud house or our plastic house or whatever we are living in, and walk around. Watch the steps at the door when you go out. It's rather dark out. Give your eyes time to adjust from the light inside to the dark outside. Let's step out, but be careful, watch your step. Don't tread on the dog shit on the sidewalk." He's very practical, very careful. He takes you out on this cold winter night, and you can hear every grass stalk covered with frozen dew crunching under your feet. Then, once you have made a relationship with your ground and your vision has adjusted to that kind of night light—maybe it is a new moon and there is no moonlight—then the stars appear very bright. There may be occasional clouds at the edges of the horizon, but there is the star of Bethlehem shining, shivering because of the cold weather.

So the spiritual friend's role is to take you out for a walk to look at the star of Bethlehem. "Take a look. We are going to go out *there*. Our trip begins tomorrow. Maybe we should walk or maybe we should drive or fly or take a train to see the star. Whatever." Then you get a personal experience, which is mutual between you and the spiritual friend, and then you have a goal, the idea that you want to get to the star of Bethlehem, enlightenment. It is a real experience at that point, no myth. It is not an optical illusion at all. There is the star of Bethlehem out there shining, and it is not a matter of conmanship at all. It's a real experience, very real. According to the Zen tradition, it is known as a satori experience. Or it can be called the meeting of two minds. A person has shown you a certain way of handling oneself, one's emotions, disciplines of all kinds. But the main point here is making enlightenment real, rather than purely a myth.

Until we've had this experience we might think, "It might work, let's take a chance." But somehow it doesn't become practical enough. We've been taking those kinds of chances for a long, long time, since we became involved in the circle of samsara. We thought we were going to be made happy one day through our striving, speeding, trying to grasp, trying to create a comfortable nest. We have done all kinds of guesswork, and we are hoping still. We never gave up hope. But somehow it actually didn't work. It wasn't a brilliant scheme, shall we say. It was rather a dumb and stupid one, in fact. We can't blame the historians or the philosophers or the scientists, particularly, or the creator of this universe. We can't even blame ourselves. It happened by accident, through karmic chain reactions. So let us not take a vengeful attitude toward anybody: "My mother messed up my life; my father messed up my life." Those blamings and pathetic gestures are becoming old hat and unreasonable. So back to square one. Meet a spiritual friend who shows you the star of

Bethlehem, enlightenment, and then start the journey immediately.

Here the sense of being is that having shared a mutual experience with your spiritual friend, there is something taking place. That's the sense of being. Whether that sense of being is created artificially or very naturally and organically doesn't really matter. It is an experience already. It *is* an experience in any case. Let's not question its validity from a metaphysical point of view or philosophically, scientifically, or domestically. We don't have time to make sure, to get a signature on the dotted line, to take out an insurance policy. And it is not only that we don't have time, but there is something more than that. This is not a business transaction. It is personal experience.

If you are a mother who has borne a child and the child is starving, you cannot blame your child, your infant, saying, "It's because you didn't bring any money along with you when you were born." That would be absurd: "We are starving because you didn't bring any money along with you." It is a karmic situation that is taking place, all along, throughout the whole thing. We are confused, utterly, as far as we know. We are confused to the point where sometimes we don't even know that. But we are confused in any case. Trying to find out who we can blame our confusion on is a further act of confusion. That takes us away from the practice of the actual discipline of meditative training, just takes us away from it.

It boils down to this: nobody has fucked up your life, really. The only thing that fucks up your life is that you actually feel somebody has pulled a trick on you or that you have pulled a trick on yourself. And as a matter of fact, there's no you. You don't even exist, you don't exist at all. So nobody's pulling a trick on anybody. Even you don't exist. You are just a myth, a mythical truth.

Within that understanding of mythical truth, we practice meditation. We sit at the level of the myth of freedom. That might be a myth—the star of Bethlehem might be a myth—but we have seen it, we have experienced it.

So you need enormous discipline, committing yourself to a spiritual friend and committing yourself, because of the spiritual friend, to yourself. And sitting practice provides an enormous help. You can't even begin to call yourself a follower of buddhadharma if no basic training of the mind is involved. In order to perceive buddha and dharma, one has to have devotion. In order to have devotion, one has to train to develop devotion. This may be very clumsy at the beginning, but it is necessary. Starting with the hinayana level of discipline, satipatthana and vipashyana practice is extremely important and powerful. It is absolutely necessary if you want to follow the path properly, thoroughly, and completely. Enlightenment is very complete, total. There's no such thing as fake enlightenment. It's real experience. It's real life.

STUDENT: You said that even we don't exist, we're a myth. Is enlightenment also a myth?
TRUNGPA RINPOCHE: You. You don't exist. Nor I. I don't exist.
S: Does enlightenment exist?
TR: Not even enlightenment exists.
S: Does devotion exist?
TR: Devotion is knowing that you don't exist. It's the information that someone gives you that you don't exist. And you experience that, that it's true: "I don't exist." That's the act of devotion. Devotion is language, media to communicate that message. Devotion acts as a mailman who brings you mail.

STUDENT: You talk about having a personal experience of the teacher, the enlightenment experience. But what I've understood you to say about enlightenment is that it isn't an experience. So what's happening at that moment? Is it enlightenment, or is it still an experience? Is there still somebody there experiencing something?
TRUNGPA RINPOCHE: Enlightenment is no longer regarded as experience. Experience is like blotting paper that absorbs ink. The blotting paper has a good experience by absorbing the ink. This requires two entities to

work together. But in this case, it is not experience from that point of view. It is total. The notion of a razor blade cutting itself.

S: If it was total at that moment, why would it end?

TR: It doesn't end, that's the whole point. Enlightenment is eternal. It doesn't end. I mean that's the whole point of liberation—once you are liberated, it is forever.

S: So the experience with the spiritual friend is just a glimpse—

TR: A glimpse of that freedom.

S: And if you went to see your spiritual friend and wanted to surrender your ego to him and didn't have a glimpse, was that because—

TR: You're still wrapped up in the notion of freedom. The whole thing about the glimpse seems to be very simple.

STUDENT: Enlightenment doesn't begin either, right?

TRUNGPA RINPOCHE: What do you mean by that?

S: It doesn't end because it doesn't begin.

TR: Well, that in itself is a beginning. Because it doesn't end, it doesn't begin, and it *is*.

STUDENT: If I don't exist, why bother?

TRUNGPA RINPOCHE: I beg your pardon?

S: If I don't exist and enlightenment doesn't exist, why bother trying to . . . I don't have the right words . . . why bother?

TR: That is the sixty-dollar question. (It has gone down

in value.) Everybody's asking that: "Why bother?" But in order to find out why you should bother, you have to find out why not? That problem hasn't been solved. As long as the twelve *nidanas*—the links in the karmic chain reactions—continue to exist. . . .

STUDENT: In some of the Tibetan literature I've read in translation, I ran across one phrase that really stuck in my mind. "The attainment of human birth is a mighty opportunity that is not to be frittered away." Could you comment on that in the light of what has just been said about nonexistence and why bother?

TRUNGPA RINPOCHE: It's very simple. This life is very valuable. Human birth is very important. You have a chance to practice, a chance to learn the truth, and still the question of "Why bother?" keeps cropping up again and again. You see, the path actually consists of "Who am I? What am I? What is this? What isn't this?" all the time until enlightenment is actually achieved. The question "Why bother?" has never been answered. It becomes one of the mantras of the path. "Why bother?" goes on all the time.

STUDENT: You said that enlightenment was a real experience and also said that enlightenment doesn't exist.

TRUNGPA RINPOCHE: Because it doesn't exist, therefore it's real. When something exists personally, experientially, and unconditionally, it becomes a mirage, fake. A lot of people maybe find that the experience they have at Disneyland is more real than the experience they have in their city life. The mirage seems to be more real.

STUDENT: It's like a mirror. You think the mirror is real.

TRUNGPA RINPOCHE: You are real in the mirror, that's right. But that still is the mirror's interpretation of you. And therefore it doesn't exist. But nonexistence is the most valid thing of all. The highest existence is nonexistence.

STUDENT: So enlightenment as a real experience is just a mirror.

TRUNGPA RINPOCHE: More than a mirror. A super-mirror. That's why in tantric language, we speak of mirrorlike wisdom—the real experience of nonexistence. Cutting through all kinds of conceptualizations and everything. The experience of vajralike *samadhi*.

STUDENT: What does making friends with yourself mean?[5]

TRUNGPA RINPOCHE: That you are very rich, re-sourceful, and that there is a working basis in you, working bases of all kinds. That you don't have to re-form yourself or abandon yourself, but work with your-self. That your passion, aggression, ignorance, and everything is workable, part of the path.

STUDENT: Are you talking about self, oneself, selves?

TRUNGPA RINPOCHE: There's no self.

S: So you're working with thought?

TR: There's no thought. There's *is*. Thoughts are interpretations of what *is*, spokesmen of nonexistence. The clouds exist because the sky exists. The sky exists because there's light that shows us blue sky. But once you get out to outer space, you don't even see blue sky. You don't even see clouds anymore.

STUDENT: If there's no self, how do we really make friends with it?

TRUNGPA RINPOCHE: Because of that. Since there's no self, there's no threat. You are not threatened by anything, because you don't exist. Therefore the world is a bank of compassion.

S: So everything is all right?

TR: So to speak.

STUDENT: You said hope was very necessary. Usually you talk about giving up hope and encourage us to adopt hopelessness. And I actually experience that the more I hope, the less I'm able to breathe. It's like if I have a lot of hope, I can't even move, because I'm so afraid I won't get what I'm hoping for. I'm so concentrated on getting something. It seems only when I give up hope, just for a minute, that I have any choice or any room.

TRUNGPA RINPOCHE: Well, giving up hope is also an act of hope. You have been encouraged to take that path of hopelessness, so it is actually more of an encouragement.

STUDENT: Does energy exist or love exist? Or are they just myths?

TRUNGPA RINPOCHE: I hope they exist. Better if they exist. But maybe they don't exist. Maybe love doesn't exist, but it *is.* Love is. Energy is. Rather than "exist." It's the same kind of distinction as: if you don't exist, you are. If energy doesn't exist, energy is. If love doesn't exist, love is.

STUDENT: How does one work on oneself?

TRUNGPA RINPOCHE: One just begins at the beginning. It's very simple. There's no how. When you ask how you should do things, it's like trying to buy a pair of gloves, so you don't have to touch, so you don't have to stress your hands. One doesn't have to think about how, one just does it.

STUDENT: Rinpoche, if there's no self, no enlightenment, no thought, and no memories, then how is it that you're able to tell us what you've experienced and what you know?

TRUNGPA RINPOCHE: Because they don't exist. Seriously. Because things don't exist, things *are.* In fact, actually it might be more correct dharmically to say, things *is.* It's not quite grammatical, but things is. There's enormous clarity out of nonexistence.

S: What perceives that nonexistence?
TR: By itself.

STUDENT: It came to me that all the three yanas are happening simultaneously. So then, does one have to isolate the hinayana from the mahayana and vajrayana in order to reach the goal of the hinayana?

TRUNGPA RINPOCHE: I think it would be safer, much safer to begin at the hinayana level, because we need a lot of training. A lot of students have to start with the path of accumulation, which is the level of the ordinary person. At that level, just learning to be an ordinary person plays an important part. That's the starting point, and one has to start in one place at a time. It's like having to chew properly before you swallow. Of course, if you chew efficiently, maybe you can chew and swallow at the same time, but that depends on your experience.

S: Is it possible, though the hinayana is where one starts and that is one's focus, that the rest may be happening anyhow, though that is not one's concern?

TR: Anyhow, yes. There is a star of Bethlehem anyhow. There is enlightenment. It actually does exist, and people have achieved it. It is real. You could experience it.

STUDENT: What is the difference between the hopelessness you have described previously and the hope that you talk about now?

TRUNGPA RINPOCHE: Same.

Well, friends, we should close our seminar. I have to go out to New Jersey and perform a wedding at a Jewish country club. But before I go, I would like to emphasize that it is worthwhile to think very seriously about the fact that if you are interested in treading the path of meditation practice, before you learn any gimmicks, you have to get yourself together. Renunciation and desolateness and aloneness or loneliness is very all-pervading. But at the same time, you cannot have a sense of renunciation, a sense of the spiritual path, without that openness of crisp, clear, winter-morning air. From the point of view of openness, meditation is not regarded as either particularly pleasurable or particularly painful. And by no means is it regarded as a magic trick that will give you instant enlightenment or instant bliss. It is a very manual experience, a very personal experience. One has to explore. One has to sit and discipline oneself constantly, all the time. Which occupies twenty-four hours of one's day.

I would like to mention that I have written a book called *Cutting Through Spiritual Materialism,* and it is worthwhile getting that book, which is a kind of extended seminar of the type we have had here. A lot is written there about what we have discussed, and it is particularly suited for a Western audience. Another very powerful book is *The Hundred Thousand Songs of Milarepa,* translated by Garma C. C. Chang. Also the late Suzuki Roshi of Zen Center in San Francisco has written a book, *Zen Mind, Beginner's Mind,* which is a very powerful book, very direct, very domesticated, very personal experience. His is a fatherly voice of some kind, which is very powerful and important. My other book *Meditation in Action,* like *Zen Mind, Beginner's Mind,* tries to communicate very simple ideas to people about the spiritual path. Also, if you have further interest in the techniques of shamatha, vipashyana, and satipatthana, there is a book called *Heart of Buddhist Meditation* by Nyanaponika Thera.

It is very necessary to do these readings to establish a knowledge of the fundamentals of buddhadharma. People in the past have worked hard and put a real and definite effort into their practice, their discipline. They have worked very hard for you people, ourselves. We should appreciate those people who worked hard on their discipline in order to be able transmit energy and wisdom to us. They are worthy of admiration. Thank you.

# PART TWO

# Barnet, Vermont
# September 1974

# 1

# *Me-ness and the Emotions*

We are going to discuss the meaning of "awake," which is connected with the practice of vipashyana, or insight, meditation. As a starting point, in order to work with the process of meditation, we have to understand our basic psychological makeup. That could be a long story, but to be concise at this point, let us say that mind has two aspects. One aspect is cognition. That is to say, there is a sense of split between I and other, me and you. This basic sense of split helps us to identify who we are, what we are. Conveniently, we are given names—I am called John, or I am called Michael, and so forth. In general we have no idea beyond the names. The names given to us are so convenient that we don't have to think behind them. We just accept ourselves as being named so-and-so. If someone asks you, "Who are you?" and you say, "I am Tom," that's regarded as a very smart answer, and usually nobody asks, "Well, who and what is Tom?" But if you are asked further questions, the next thing you go to is, "I am a banker" or "I am a cab driver." You shift to your profession. You end up jumping back and forth among those external identifications, and usually you never get back to the "me" level. That's the way we usually handle our life. But this time we are going to go beyond the names to the basic mind. We are actually going to find out who we are and what we are. This is the starting point for understanding the mind.

Our mind has this quality of "me-ness," which is obviously not the other, not you. Me-ness is distinct from you, other, the rock, the tree, or the mountains, the rivers, the sky, the sun, the moon—what have you. This me-ness is the basic point here.

There is a general sense of discomfort when you refer to yourself as "me," which is a very subtle discomfort. We usually don't acknowledge or notice it, because it is so subtle, and since it is there all the time, we become immune to it. There is a certain basic ambivalence there. It is like dogs, who at a certain point begin to relate to their leashes as providing security rather than imprisonment. Animals in the zoo feel the same thing. At the beginning they experienced imprisonment, but at some point this became a sense of security. We have the same kind of attitude. We have imprisoned ourselves in a certain way, but at the same time, we feel that this imprisonment is the most secure thing we have. This me-ness or my-ness has a painful quality of imprisonment, but at the same time, it also represents security rather than just pure pain. That is the situation we are in at this point. Every one of us is in that situation.

This me-ness is not painful in the sense of outright suffering, like what you get from eating a bottle of jalapeño chili peppers. But there's something behind the whole thing that makes us very subtly nauseated, just a little bit. That nausea then becomes somewhat sweet, and we get hooked on that sweetness. Then if we lose our nausea, we also lose our sweet. That is the basic state of mind that everybody feels.

When the first of the four noble truths talks about suffering, this is what it is talking about. There is that very subtle but at the same time very real and very personal thing going on, which sort of pulls us down. Of course there are various occasions when you might feel on top of the world. You have a fantastic vacation by the ocean or in the mountains. You fall in love or you celebrate a success in your career. You find something positive to hang on to. Nobody can deny that every one of us has experienced that kind of glory. But at the same time that we are experiencing that high point of glory, the other end of the canoe, so to speak, is pushed down into the water a bit. That big deal that we are trying to make into a small deal continues to happen. Sometimes when it comes up on the surface, we call it depression. We think, "I feel bad, I feel sick, I feel terrible, I feel upset," and so forth. But at the same time, it is really something less than that. There is a basic, fundamental hangover, an all-pervasive hangover that is always taking place. Even though we may be feeling good about things, we have the sense of being stuck somewhere.

Often people interpret that sense of being stuck in such a way that they can blame it on having to put up with their parents' hang-ups, or on hang-ups resulting from some other part of their problematic case history. You had a bad experience, you say, therefore, this hang-up exists. People come up with these very convenient case-historical interpretations, maybe even bringing in physical symptoms. These are the very convenient escapes that we have.

But really there is something more than that involved, something that transcends one's case history. We do feel something that goes beyond parents, beyond a bad childhood, a bad birth, a difficult cesarean—whatever. There is something beyond all that taking place, a basic fuckedupedness that is all-pervasive. What Buddha calls it is ego, or neurosis.

That is the first of the two aspects of the mind we mentioned. It's something we carry with us all the time. I'm afraid it is rather depressing.

The second aspect of mind, which comes out of this one, is what is popularly known as emotions. This includes emotions of all types, such as lust, hatred, jealousy, pride, fear—all kinds of things. However, the word *emotion* is questionable. By calling them emotions we come to look at them as something special, "my emotions," which brings a rather unhealthy way of looking at ourselves. We think, "If only I could get rid of my emotions, my outrageousness, then I could function peacefully and beautifully." But somehow that never happens. Nobody has yet achieved a state without emotions and still had a functioning mind.

From the Buddhist point of view, this second aspect of mind is not emotion as such; rather these eruptions that occasionally take place in our mind also are regarded as thoughts. They are part of the thinking process; they are a heavier instance of the thinking process, rather than a phenomenon of a different type, as though there were a special disease, like smallpox or something, called emotions. They are just a heavy-handed flu.

This first aspect of mind is mainly occupied with duality, the basic split, the sense of being fundamentally alone. This second aspect goes beyond that; it is highly occupied, extremely active. It produces daydreams and dreams and memories and stores them in the "akashic records," or whatever you would like to call it.[6] It stores them all over the place, and it reopens them and reexplores them whenever we run out of material, whenever we have a conflict or a confrontation with the other. We are constantly trying to work out our relation to the other. It's like your dog meeting somebody else's dog. There is a growl, a sniff, a step forward, a potential rejection, or maybe an acceptance. That kind of thing is constantly taking place. Dogs do it very generously. As far as we human beings are concerned, obviously we are more subtle, but we are less generous because we have more me. But still this process goes on constantly—we do that when we confront our world.

This cannot just be called emotion; it is something greater, more overall. The thought process escalates to a level of high intensity—so-called emotion. But this second mental faculty is actually a confrontation process, a communication process that goes on all the time. And that confrontation and communication consists of thought patterns alone—nothing else. Sometimes your thought looks, sometimes your thought speaks, sometimes your thought listens, sometimes your thought smells, sometimes your thought feels. It's a thought process that takes place.

This is also connected with the process of sense perception. According to the Buddhist tradition, there is a sixth kind of sense perception, which is actually mental. It is the fickleness of mind, the sixth sense, which acts as the switchboard that all the wires come into—from your ears, from your nose, your eyes, your tongue, your body. These sense organs report their messages to the central headquarters, the switchboard, and the switchboard delegates certain activities by way of response.

So that is basically the way the whole mental process works, which does not give us any grounds for separating thought process from emotions. All these aspects are part of the same process that takes place.

In studying vipashyana, we are going to discuss dealing with those thought processes in the practice of meditation. But first it is necessary for you to understand the basic ground, what the basic mechanism is: who is going to meditate, and what we are going to meditate with. We are going to be talking about the way of working with thoughts, with the second aspect of mind. We have very little resources at this point for working with the first aspect of mind, the basic fucked-upedness. That mentality of dualism, or the split, cannot be handled directly, I'm afraid. But hopefully it can be uplifted by dealing with its products.

We could say that the thought process, including the so-called emotions, is like the branches of a tree. By cutting step by step through the elaborate setup of the branches, we come to the root, and at that point the root will not be difficult to deal with. So the thought process seems to be our starting point.

You might say, "Wouldn't a good strategist cut the root first?" Obviously, he would; but we are not in a position to do so. Actually, if we started by trying to struggle with the root, the branches would keep on growing, and we would be completely and helplessly engulfed by the rampant growth of the branches and the fruits dropping on our heads.

So Buddha's psychological approach is a different

one. We start dealing with the leaves and branches. Then once we have dealt with that, we have some kind of realization of the naked truth, of the reality of the basic split. Then we begin to realize the first noble truth, which says that the truth is suffering, the truth is that hang-up, that problem.[7]

In order to understand the first noble truth, we have to understand how to live with "emotions." We will have a certain amount of time to discuss that in this present seminar. Now perhaps we could have a discussion.

STUDENT: We start work with what we normally think of as emotions, with the thought process as a whole, which is the branches and leaves of the trees. And the cognitive process is more the root, which we get to later?

TRUNGPA RINPOCHE: That's right. In order to scrub the floor, first we have to clean it off. Once you clean it off, you know what you are doing. It's a reasonable way of handling the whole thing. You start with what you have immediately available, which brings you an enormous contact with reality. Whereas if you were to try to relate to the basic duality, you would just find it impossible. Instead of trying to work brick by brick, it would be like trying to push down a whole wall. You would end up with a defeat. So it's better to start with small things that are quite pronounced rather than starting with the fundamental subtleties and trying to sort out the whole problem.

STUDENT: Do these fundamental subtleties come up disguised as fantasies?

TRUNGPA RINPOCHE: They are more or less the same thing as the fantasies, but they can't really be disguised. The root of a tree can't be disguised as the leaves. The root has to remain the root in order to hold up the leaves and branches. The basic subtleties act as a sustainer, so they have to keep their position.

STUDENT: Emotions are accompanied by physical sensations. Are those also thoughts?

TRUNGPA RINPOCHE: Yes. That does not mean to say that you don't feel physically, but your body is also your thought. For example, if you cut your finger while you're chopping an onion, you have a bleeding thought. But it's real. Thoughts shouldn't be dismissed as "just thoughts." Such a thought is so real, it's tangible.

STUDENT: Would you mind clarifying those two aspects of mind again? The first one is characterized as the basic duality between me and the other; and the second one, a worse case, involves intense thoughts. Is that right?

TRUNGPA RINPOCHE: It's quite simple. The first one is basic duality, and the second one is the activities of that.

S: Can they be separated as a first form of thought and then a second?

TR: They are not the first or second thoughts, but the roots and the branches.

S: The first one is the root.

TR: Yes.

S: So we have to get at the root through the branches.

TR: Yes, we have to start with the branches first.

S: So when we see through the very highly differentiated thoughts and sensations that we're involved with, then we come to the more fundamental thing between self and other.

TR: Yes. If you start by tackling the self and other, in tackling that you start more branches, so you have an endless job.

S: I see.

TR: Anyway, that's what we said.

STUDENT: I grasp what you're saying abstractly, but I'm wanting to put it into some experiential framework so it's not just an abstract idea.

TRUNGPA RINPOCHE: Well, that's why you are here, obviously. We will discuss the details in the coming talks. To begin with, I wanted to make clear what subject we would be discussing and give you a basic map. That might be somewhat abstract or not particularly pragmatic at this point.

STUDENT: Is the sixth sense you mentioned related to intuition?

TRUNGPA RINPOCHE: It's a lot of things—intuition, paranoia, hope and fear—all kinds of things. Intuition is included, but in this case intuition has some kind of a reference point. Therefore you have intuition that is different from the enlightened kind of intuition, which is wisdom. Here this is intuition on a very crude level.

# 2

# *Recollecting the Present*

The basic approach to understanding the mind is a process of gradually making friends with oneself. That is the first step.

At first, we feel what we are and what we have is somewhat chaotic, and we feel alienated from ourselves. One sterile approach of traditional spirituality is to play heavily on one's inadequacy, one's weakness. You are encouraged to recognize that more and more, until you reach the point where you can't actually stand yourself. You get involved in all kinds of self-flagellation, self-blame. You feel poverty-stricken. You are filled with a sense of how bad you are, how badly you behave—how fucked up you are, basically. This is the trick that is played on you by some forms of traditional spirituality.

People in certain evangelical traditions, who are particularly interested in converting people to their faith, make use of this trick to make their teachings seem more glorious. They are unable to raise their doctrines or teachings any higher or make them any deeper or more direct and personal, so instead of raising the level of consciousness or of the doctrinal or meditative understanding of their teaching, they choose to lower the other area—that of the people they are dealing with. They reduce them lower and lower—to the level of sewage. Through doing that, their own level automatically seems to become higher, more impressive.

So they play on your guilt and your weakness and whatever emotional fuckedupedness exists in you. They tell you that if you keep going the way you are, you are going to get worse, you are already worse, you could get even worse than that, and eventually you will be no more than a turd if you don't pull yourself together.

That is the kind of trick that has been played on people—which is by no means meditative or connected with spiritual practice in any way. It is a kind of spiritual-materialistic way of inspiring someone to embark on the spiritual path: to reduce them to nothing.

The approach of meditation is the opposite of that. In that approach, we give people a chance at least. At least we provide some kind of a handle or stepping-stone. There is a working base, there are possibilities, there is inspiration. There is something happening within one's state of being, which is meditation practice.

Nevertheless, the approach of meditation is not all that easy. You've got to do it yourself. The teachers and the teachings can only show you how to do it, that's the closest we can come. But then you have to do it yourself. You can't expect complete hospitality. Your car can only go as far as the garage; it can't drive you into the bedroom. Once your car has stopped in the garage, you have to walk to the bedroom; you have to take off your clothes, you have to get in bed. A certain effort is involved. No matter how tired and how helpless you are, the hospitality offered by your transportation doesn't carry you beyond that. Unless you fall asleep in your car, which often happens, both metaphorically and in actual fact.

So students are given as much assistance as possible, which consists in showing them the path. Showing the path in a down-to-earth, practical way is traditionally known as "grandmother's finger pointing." The grandmother is old and wise and knows how to handle the details of life, and she points with her finger and tells you to do this and this and this. "Grandmother's finger pointing" is a particular term of the Kagyü tradition of Buddhism in Tibet. Showing you how to do it in this way is the closest we can get to helping you along the path.

But there is a need for some acknowledgment and some willingness on the part of the student. You have to be willing to follow the grandmother's finger pointing. If that is the case, then the next question is quite obviously, what are we going to do? The answer is, practice meditation.

There are two types of meditation practice. One is called *shamatha*, which means "development of peace." The other is called *vipashayana*, which means "development of insight." We discussed that in basic outline in the last talk. We cannot develop complete vipashyana unless we have some background as to what shamatha is all about. In terms of the metaphor of the tree we used earlier, shamatha is not cutting the branches or leaves of the tree. That comes much later. Before we do that, we have to acknowledge the basic tree*ness*—the branchness, the leafness—how the whole setup is seen and experienced. That is an important prerequisite for vipashyana. We can't skip that point. We must discuss that before we discuss vipashyana, the development of insight.

In shamatha, there is a meditative technique, which involves working on a natural resource—breath, your breathing. We start with your breathing. That is always available, as long as you are alive. You always have your breath as you always have your heartbeat, whether you are excited or you are asleep or you are in a normal state. You always have to breathe.

Your breathing is the closest you can come to a picture of your mind. It is the portrait of your mind in some sense. It goes in and goes out—it sort of fertilizes itself so that the next breath can take place. It is not a stationary object. It moves and it stops and it moves again. It sustains the body; it is a source of life. Also it is the source of your speech and the source of your thinking. If your heartbeat stops, your breath stops, you can't think, you drop dead. So the breath is a statement of life and a statement of the mind at the same time. In order to eat, to smell food and chew it, you have to breathe. If you're tired, you breathe heavier. If you're relaxed, you breathe easy. If your neck is bent, you snore. If your sleeping posture is straight, you don't snore. When you are hungry, you breathe in a special way; when you're full, you breathe in a special way; when you feel happy, you breathe in a special way; when you feel sad, you breathe in a special way. Breath is changing constantly, but at the same time it constantly keeps its rhythm. Breath, which is yearning for space, stops at the end of the out-breath. By surrendering the breath, the yearning for space, at the end of the out-breath, you get more space. Therefore you can live longer—you can take the next breath. You have two kinds of space. There is the outer space as you breathe out. And before you breathe in, there's a gap. You breathe in outer space, and then as you breathe in, you have another kind of space, which is the inner space within your bodily system. Then you have a gap and then you breathe out again. So there is action, stillness, action, stillness taking place constantly. Which is the portrait of your mind.

Therefore the breath is chosen as the basis for working on your practice of meditation. Working with the breath is recommended. The breath is not separate from you, but on the other hand, it is not quite you. Thus there are enigmatic qualities to the breath. And the same goes for your mind. Is your mind *your* mind? Maybe. But then what is you is uncertain. So we never actually come to a conclusion as to who is who or what is who. We just constantly hope for the best. Hopefully, we could survive, we could continue in this vague way.

You might be extremely articulate and precise and sharp, but still you have no idea where all this comes from, where all this goes. But the basic point here is just that the state of mind has to match with the breath, you have to relate with the breath. In the beginning stage of shamatha, you work with your breath, you don't concentrate on your mind. That is impossible to do. Actually, concentrating on your breath is also impossible, because your breathing shifts and changes, and so does your mind. So in connection with shamatha we prefer to use the word *mindfulness* rather than *concentration*.

Concentration has certain connotations. The idea seems to be that you focus on a particular object or a particular subject until you develop a complete photographic relationship with it; and then you can let go and the concentrated state of mind remains. This is very tiresome and very specialized and too industrious in some sense. Therefore Buddhist textbooks say that *concentration* is a dangerous word to use in connection with the practice of meditation. Instead we refer to this practice as mindfulness.

If you are fully with your mind, you could be there, on the spot. But at the same time, you do not have to focus your whole system on one point of reference. In fact there is a very interesting dichotomy here, which comes from the fact that you have no understanding who *you* are. You don't know who *you* are. You haven't even got a clue, or that is the clue. Maybe we could use the clue as you. But that is as far as we get, rather than getting to the actuality of what *you* is all about. Therefore you cannot concentrate *your* mind. The closest you can come is to be mindful, mind full. The very vague state that exists, known as consciousness, has never seen itself, but it is there. It has never felt itself, but it moves, it happens. Now that state of what we call mind can be full. We can be mind full.

The Buddhist scriptures talk about resting or abiding in recollection. The best English equivalent of this is *mindfulness*. "Recollection" in this case does not mean dwelling on the past but being in the present. That flow that takes place—you could be with it.

Our present state of mind is based on a reference point. Without a reference point we can't think, we can't eat, we can't sleep, we can't behave. We have to have some reference point as to how to eat, when to stop eating, how to walk, when to stop walking, how to conduct our life—which way? this way, that way, the other way, some other way altogether. All those choices are guided by a reference point. "This is good to do, therefore I am doing this; this is not good to do, therefore I am doing that." There are choices upon choices taking place constantly. Attending to those choices and their reference points is known as recollection, *smriti* in Sanskrit. This is not exactly bringing the past to the present, but still in order to be in the present, you need memory, which is an automatic thing.

Our mind functions that way usually—in terms of reference point, which equals memory. In making your body function, there are reference points all the time: stretching your arm, lifting your cup and bringing it toward your mouth, tilting it a little bit, drinking, then tasting and swallowing. As you lift and stretch your arm, you do not forget to hold the cup. There is a coordination taking place, which is entirely based on memory. Without that we can't function. On that basis we have developed certain behavior patterns, which make it possible for us to handle our lives. This coordination enables body and mind to be synchronized. And that synchronicity is based on a recollection of the present. Recollecting the present in this way is called being mindful. Mind in this case is equal to recollection. Being mindful is being there, fully minded. If you have a full mind, you have a full reference point. Therefore you are *there*. You relate directly to the present situation, which is precisely what meditation—shamatha practice—is all about. Just being there, very simply, directly; conducting yourself very precisely, relating very thoroughly and fully.

The reference point in shamatha is the breath. The traditional recommendation of the lineage of meditators that developed in the Kagyü-Nyingma tradition is based on the idea of mixing mind and breath. This means that you should be with the breath, you *are* the breath. Your breath goes out and you go out. Your breath dissolves into the atmosphere and you dissolve into the atmosphere. Then you just let go completely. You even forget meditation practice at that point. You just let go. There is a gap. Then naturally, automatically, physiologically, you breathe in. Let that be the gap. Then you breathe out again. Out, dissolve, gap. Go out again, dissolve, there's a gap. Go out, dissolve, there's a gap. You continue to proceed in that way.

There is a moment of space, the gap. We could say there's a moment of weakness, if you like. The whole thing should not be too heroic. And then when you relate with the out-breath, there is a moment of strength. Then the moment of weakness: you dissolve, you have nothing to hang on to. Then you pick up doing something again—going out with the out-breath.

That is the basic technique of shamatha. It has to be very precise and direct.

Then there is walking meditation, which has also

been recommended. You walk mindfully. You pay heed to, say, your right leg. As your weight shifts, the pressure releases, and the weight is put on the left leg. So your right leg is free, and then you lift it off the ground, swing it. Then it touches the ground, presses the ground as your weight is put on it, and your left leg is released. That is also very precise. One does not have to walk like a zombie in order to do that. You walk with a reasonable natural rhythm; let it be natural, just as with the breath. When you walk that way, very precise decisions have to be taken: this is the time to put weight on this leg, then the other leg, and so on. So the whole process becomes very precise and very direct and very clear. At this point, you have no intention whatsoever in doing this. You are not thinking, "If I do this, I will attain enlightenment tomorrow." You have no concern about anything else but doing your practice of sitting or walking meditation.

This is what is called discipline in the Buddhist tradition and patience as well. Participating in that ongoing process without purpose behind it. Students are advised to do this in a very orthodox way, to pay full attention. But this doesn't mean that you have to be solemn or serious, particularly. If you are serious, that takes away your mindfulness. You get very busy being serious and you lose your mindfulness. Your mind has to be full, rather than one-eighth or one-hundredth. It has to be right there on the spot. We have the expression "Mind your business," which means, "Leave me alone, let me be myself." At this point you mind *your* business. Just be there, directly and simply be there.

To do that is to experience the leaves that exist on the tree. You begin to find out who you are somewhat, or who you are not. Whatever—that particular metaphysical problem doesn't matter very much at this point. We can sort that out later.

What is your mind? Students might begin to think about this. As you practice, you might come to conclusions regarding hidden emotions that begin to come up to the surface like dead fish. And you might experience all kinds of contrasts in your point of view on the world, seeing it upside down, downside up. At one point, you might feel you are on top of the world; at another point, you might feel you are at the bottom of hell. The whole time the basic point is to be very precise.

This approach is not only for the sitting practice of meditation alone, which is heavily recommended, but it also applies after the sitting practice of meditation is over, to what is called the postmeditation experience. That is to say that your life and your commitment to the practice of meditation is not a matter of a patch here and a patch there that you are trying to sew together. Your life is committed to meditation overall, like a blanket. It is from twelve o'clock to twelve o'clock. Your life is completely infested with the prac-

tice of meditation. When you are eating, you eat.
When you are washing your dishes, you are there with
it, right on the spot. It is not a matter of trying to work
with your breath and wash your dishes at the same
time, which would be cumbersome, unnecessary. In the
postmeditation, if you are washing your dishes, you do
it properly, completely, fully. Be with that; be with the
tap, with the water, be with the dirty dishes; be with
your arms, your hands, your coordination with your
mind. Be with the water and the faucet and the soap
and the sponge. Let us be them together and make a
good job of washing the dishes. It is a matter of being
on the spot with everything that way. From that point
of view, it is a life commitment, a twenty-four-hour
job.

It has been said that you can't practice meditation
without postmeditation mindfulness. Mindfulness
throughout our lives when we are not doing sitting
practice is also a part of the practice of meditation. One
has to have some kind of self-consciousness in order to
lead one's life properly, to be meditative.

Often the term *self-consciousness* is used pejoratively,
which is not fair. Or we could say that there are different kinds of self-consciousness. One idea is that self-
consciousness has to do with feeling guilty, feeling
hurt, feeling pain. But that is not the kind of self-consciousness we are talking about. That kind of self-
consciousness is a punishment to oneself. But that is

more than self-consciousness. That is heavy-handed egotism. Something else is taking place there. The kind of self-consciousness we talk about in relation to awareness or mindfulness is just being yourself, simply. You possess two arms, you have a sink, you have dirty dishes, and you do a good job. Not for the sake of doing a good job. You just do it, and it turns out to be a good job by accident. That kind of self-consciousness is no problem. It is a way of handling yourself properly, being yourself. Once you take that kind of attitude, you just do it.

It's not a matter of being a great meditator who does a beautiful job of washing up. It's without praise, without blame. As long as there is a notion of trying to prove something, you have the painful kind of self-consciousness, self-consciousness in the pejorative sense. That is the case as long as you're concerned about the end product. "Look what a beautiful job I did. That's because I studied and meditated."

That is the kind of problem that a lot of Zen students fall into. There is some problem having to do with a sense of showmanship. "We sit and therefore we do a good job. Come to Zen!" It's like every Zen student is a self-existing Zen advertisement.

The basic point is to be precise and direct and without aim. Be there precisely. There is a need for mindfulness, which is the equivalent of self-consciousness, if you like—light-handed self-consciousness, which does exist. As long as we feel we exist—which we don't, but never mind about that problem; we actually don't exist, but we think we do, and that provides us with a working basis; we don't have to start 100 percent pure—as long as we feel we exist, let us be full. Let us begin that way. That seems to be the basic point for the practice of meditation. If I say too much, probably you'll be confused, so let's stop there.

STUDENT: When we speak of postmeditation awareness, does that mean we should try to be more aware or that it happens spontaneously because of meditation?

TRUNGPA RINPOCHE: One *does* try; not try-try, but just try.

S: Sounds like quite a fine line.

TR: Yes, that is what we are talking about. It is a very special way, but it does not have to be a big deal, particularly. You just have this aura that you are part of this meditation livelihood—basically, that your life is the practice of meditation. In fact, you find it difficult to shake it off. You might say, "I'm sick of the whole thing; now I'm giving up my awareness and my meditation completely." Okay, do so. But then you find that something is haunting you constantly. You gave up meditation, but there you are—you have developed more awareness, more mindfulness. That always happens to people. So this is not a matter of something being imposed on you, but there is that element of something-or-other that goes on all the time.

It's like being in the world. You are in the midst of winter and you have that awareness; awareness of that wintry quality is there all the time. If you are in New York City, you don't have to meditate on it. You don't have to develop a special awarenesss of New-York-City-ness. You pick up the New-York-ness anyhow, whether you are indoors or outdoors. There is an overall aware-ness, that you are in that particular location. So it's more of a general climate than a particular effort. But that climate has to be acknowledged occasionally. That's very important.

STUDENT: You were talking about breath and the movement of the breath being a mirror of the mind. Couldn't that be extended to the whole body? Wouldn't the movement of the whole body also be a mirror of the mind, the thought processes, and there-fore another path of meditation?

TRUNGPA RINPOCHE: Well, you could stretch in that direction, but there's a bit of a strain there.

S: I don't see that.

TR: You don't move all the time, unless you are rest-less; but you breathe all the time.

S: No. Our human bodies are designed to move almost all the time. In fact, it's almost impossible to sit per-fectly still the way we are designed with our center of gravity.

TR: I'm not trying to tell you you should fight your

center of gravity, particularly. But there are moments of stillness, relatively speaking. It is the breath that makes your body move. Your lungs always expand and contract, but that's sort of an accidental thing. The reason why meditation practice should be based just on your breath, not on your body, is that there are possibilities of exploring the parts of your body unnecessarily. You start to try to shape your body like your mind, which has a hint of neurosis in it. In fact, that happens a great deal in the sensory-awareness schools of meditation. And there has been a great interest in T'ai Chi Ch'uan that has gone along with the enormous interest in touch and bodily movement. But there is a limit on how you can do that. There is a tendency to create something special. Whereas when you just sit with the breath, you don't have to breathe specially. You just do it naturally. It's part of your pulse.

S: But since most of our time is spent in movement, why not use movement as a form of meditation?

TR: I think you can't do that. At this point I have to be very orthodox. You can't do that, because it would be very convenient and there would be no discipline. For example, you have to set aside a time for sitting practice that is especially allocated for that practice. Whereas with the approach you suggest, you could just say: "Well, I'm going to visit my girlfriend and I have to drive. So on my way to my girlfriend's I'll use driving as my meditation."

S: But as long as it's mindful, why couldn't that be done?

TR: That approach to mindfulness becomes too utilitarian, too pragmatic—killing two birds with one stone. "That way I meditate and I get a chance to see my girlfriend at the end too." But something has to be given up somewhere. Some renunciation somewhere is necessary. One stone kills one bird.

STUDENT: You talked about mindfulness and breathing, and breathing as a portrait of the mind. You also talked about being mindful of the various thoughts and feelings that come and go. You described those as the branches of the tree, which I gather is what we're supposed to attack.

TRUNGPA RINPOCHE: At this point we are not in a position to handle those, to deal with them, to cut them down. Now we just have to see that the branches do exist.

S: I'm confused about this. Is breathing the tool we are fashioning to eventually cut down the branches?

TR: No, the mindfulness.

S: The mindfulness. Of which the breathing is—

TR: The breathing is just crutches.

S: Yeah. The breathing is the crutches to bring about the mindfulness, which we can then later develop toward the emotions. Okay, that's it!

TR: That's it.

STUDENT: You say that we don't exist, that we only think we exist. I see that as being part of the grand illusion. Could you elaborate on that?

TRUNGPA RINPOCHE: That's a lengthy discussion. But maybe I could hear from you what you think about whether you exist or you don't. Do you think you exist?

S: I think that—

TR: Be honest.

S: We are here.

TR: Yes?

S: Whatever these vibrations are are here. We are here.

TR: Well, who are we?

S: Who's asking the question?

TR: That's it. Yes. Who is it. But that's no proof.

S: Does the enlightened mind perceive—

TR: It doesn't matter about the enlightened mind. Let's talk about *this* mind, samsaric mind. When we talk about enlightened mind, it tends to become a myth. You expect the enlightened mind would see rainbows all over the place. But how about us, who see garbage all over the place?

S: I'm not sure how we can exist and not exist.

TR: You don't. Where are you at this moment?

S: I'm here.

TR: What's here?

S: Planet Earth.

TR: Planet Earth. Well, that's a good beginning. What location on Planet Earth?

S: It doesn't matter.

TR: Oh, come on. You are in Vermont! We have a tent above our head and we have ground to sit on. Maybe you're sitting on a cushion to make yourself comfortable. And you're wearing a sweater so that the cold doesn't become too heavy-handed on you. So we are here, in the tent in Barnet, Vermont, Tail of the Tiger. But then who is here? I don't mean your name. Other than your name. What is here?

S: Some sort of consciousness.

TR: What is that? Consciousness of what?

S: Self-consciousness.

TR: That's just a catch phrase. What does that mean? Consciousness of what? [Pause] Don't think too much.

S: Consciousness of the breeze.

TR: What's behind the breeze?

S: My mind.

TR: What is that?

S: I wish I knew.

TR: You don't know?

S: I guess that's why I'm here.

TR: You mean that's why you're not here? [Uproarious laughter] Good luck, sir.

STUDENT: Is the problem that I do not exist, in other words, that there's nothing existing, or is the problem that something exists but it isn't I? It isn't the I that I think I am, but there is the existence of something.

TRUNGPA RINPOCHE: That's saying the same thing. Something equals nothing. If you are the number one, one necesssarily depends on zero. One is something and zero is nothing. In order to have one, you have to have zero. Which is nothing. It doesn't make any difference—something and nothing are the same. Otherwise you couldn't have a cash register. I think there's no problem with something and nothing.

On the other hand, there's something else, which is nothing that's real, but it's something that's nothing. That's where we get confused—when we're trying to figure out the whole thing. This is a long research project, and I don't think we can sort it out tonight. But you are very courageous.

STUDENT: In your previous talk, I got the impression that thoughts and emotions were dependent on duality.
TRUNGPA RINPOCHE: Yes.
S: But it seems that people who have overcome duality, saints and so on, still have thoughts and emotions.
TR: Yes.
S: Well, I think you have to bring in a third factor in order to complete the picture.
TR: Well said. So what's behind that? You didn't finish your statement.
S: Well, this is why I asked the question.
TR: Maybe that's your statement. Making things into a question is a very easy thing to do. This is part of

the problem. In fact, the question mark is a symbol of nonexistence. You write a little poem and then you send it up like a balloon into the air. Hopefully someone will catch it and appreciate it. That's a question—it goes up. But perhaps we are branching off from our basic thing.

STUDENT: I don't know if this is branching off even further, but this practice you've been describing seems very sensible in a way—becoming more aware, becoming more in touch with what's happening in your own mind and outside of you. But I wonder why tantra is necessary. Why isn't this enough, if one could eventually do it properly?

TRUNGPA RINPOCHE: I think it's a matter of attitude, actually. Tantra is not something that is there to save us from a problem. And tantra is absolutely not necessary at this point. This is a complete thing. But this thing becomes tantra eventually. You might say you always want to remain a teenager. "I have everything in my life, I know everything, I go to school and learn everything. This is my life. Why do I have to get old?" You don't have to get old, but you do become old one day. This particular experience we are talking about becomes tantra at some point, rather than tantra being imposed on you as a necessary requirement. The shamatha-vipashyana experience matures. That is tantra. It happens automatically.

S: So tantra is just sort of an exposition of what happens.

TR: Yes. That's why we can speak of the three yanas being linked together. The whole development is regarded as a maturation process rather than something that is imposed on you. Nobody says to you, "Now you are finished with hinayana, you should change to second gear and do mahayana, then change to the top gear, which is tantra." You don't ever change that way. It's a gradual process of development that becomes tantra automatically when it reaches maturity. You don't ask, "Why is it necessary to have fruit on the trees?" This particular plant is beautiful, and it's doing its best. It's necessary to look at the situation wholeheartedly at this point. And maybe that kind of looking actually could be a tantric view.

# 3

# *The Portable Stage Set*

We should probably discuss the various types of backgrounds with the help of which we operate in our lives. These backgrounds are vague, uncertain, dubious for us. I am talking about the kind of background we create in our minds in every situation—when we enter somebody's room, when we sit by ourselves, when we meet someone. This kind of background is partially made up of the sense of basic space that we carry around with us all the time, and it is also colored by our particular mood of the moment. It is a kind of portable stage set that we carry around with us that enables us to operate as individuals. We constantly produce a display, a theatrical scene. For each situation we create the appropriate backdrop and the appropriate lighting. We also have the appropriate actors, mainly ourselves, who appear on the stage. We carry on this kind of play, this theatrical game, all the time, and we are constantly using our antennae, so to speak, to feel out the total effect our stage set is having.

In vipashyana meditation, we deal with this kind of

background, our portable theater. Whether we are a big deal or a small deal, there is always some kind of a deal happening. Vipashyana works with that big deal or small deal, that great deal, large deal, littlest, expansive, cunning, or clever deal—whatever setup you have chosen to establish. In practicing vipashyana, instead of keeping very busy setting up your theater, your theatrical stage, your attitude is changed so that there is a sense of questioning how we produce this background, why we do it, whether we have to do it or might not have to do it. This is still on the level of inquiry in some sense, but at the same time it is experiential.

In vipashyana, you as the practitioner experience the game that you are playing in setting up your theater. From that you pick up a new way of dealing with the whole thing without its being a game. This is the sitting practice of meditation. When you sit, you don't sit for the sake of creating a display or a particular effect. It's a very private thing in some sense. In sitting practice, you relate to the radiation you are creating. Before you begin sitting, this radiation was being created purely in order to impress or overpower the audience. In this case, the situation is reversed. You experience your own radiation face to face rather than playing with it in order to impress or overpower your audience. You have no audience when you sit and meditate, or you are your own audience.

Even in this situation, however, it is possible for subtle little tricks to take place. You congratulate yourself for sitting and being such a good boy or good girl, and try to make that into a display. It's very subtle. The games can be peeled away one after the other like the layers of an onion. The games continue to happen, obviously, but somehow you can deal with this.

You have had the basic training of shamatha practice and from there you begin to expand. I would like to stress again that the shamatha experience is extremely important. Without that foundation, the practitioner is not at all in a position to experience vipashyana. But with that foundation, the practitioner can begin to expand the meaning of mindfulness so that it becomes awareness. Mindfulness is being fully there, and awareness is a total sensing. In awareness, all happenings are seen at once. This could also be called panoramic vision.

Panoramic vision, in this case, is having a sense of the entire radiation that we create. We possess a certain mannerism or a certain style that is reflected outward. When you sit, this becomes purely a thought process. You develop a sense of appreciation of things around you, not one by one, but totally. It's like light radiating from a flame or a light bulb that expands outward. However, we find that this radiation has no radiat*or*. If you look into who is doing all these tricks, producing this display, this radiation, there is nobody. Even the *idea* of somebody doesn't exist. There is a pure sense of openness, a sense that you can relate with the living world as an open world.

At this point, we are only just introducing the vipashyana experience. Later we will go into it in greater detail. What it is necessary to understand now is that the vipashyana experience does not proceed to the level of a game, but remains purely at the level of experience, the living experience of awareness (as opposed to mindfulness).

Awareness, in this case, is not awareness of self but awareness of the other. The difference between the two is that if you are aware of yourself, it is awareness of yourself being aware of yourself aware of yourself aware of yourself aware of yourself. There is some kind of incest taking place. Whereas, if you are just being aware, that is openness, a welcoming gesture. You include your doings within your realm of awareness, so you don't punish or you don't watch. You don't question, particularly, but you just be. That seems to be the basic approach or the basic policy in insight meditation, vipashyana.

Do you understand what I've been saying?

STUDENT: I don't understand about the radiation without a radiator.

TRUNGPA RINPOCHE: If you have a radiator, the radiator has to work itself up to the level where there is enough radiation to be expanded or reflected outward.

It remains tied up with that, so there is really no radiation.

S: Doesn't radiation cease to exist if there is no radiator?

TR: Radiation can only exist if there is no radiator. Things can only flow if the flow is the process that's happening rather than somebody instigating the flow. Then it's deadly.

STUDENT: You said that awareness is not awareness of self but of other. Do you mean that the actions and reactions coming from oneself have no greater priority or value than what seems to be occurring in the outside world? That it's all one field?

TRUNGPA RINPOCHE: Awareness of other is the same idea as radiation without a radiator. Awareness takes place, and that awareness is 100 percent all by itself. There is no need for you to watch your awareness as a careful speculator or instigator. One of the problems is, if you have a very efficient instigator, then your product is killed. That's the kind of self-existing suicide that takes place all the time, which is known as neurosis.

STUDENT: So if you have a man standing by a mountain, his awareness would be purely of the mountain.

TRUNGPA RINPOCHE: Yes. He's not important, because the mountain is around him.

STUDENT: If you draw attention to the mountain as opposed to the self, you are assuming that there is still a self to be gotten rid of. I thought that a truly open awareness would be directed toward the mutuality of this self and the other, or their mutual nonexistence. I can't see singling out the other at the expense of the self or vice versa. Isn't that giving a sort of negative importance to the self?

TRUNGPA RINPOCHE: I don't think there's any problem there, particularly. You could be open to the mountain and see the mountain more freely without you. On the other hand, if you have a stomach upset or a headache and at the same time are trying to look at the mountain to cheer yourself up, you somehow have a problem trying to maintain your suffering and trying to look at the mountain. You have a complete experience neither of your headache nor of the mountain.

STUDENT: But I always have something going on like a headache. I never have a perfect condition for just looking outward. There's always something going on with me. I may feel joyful, for example, and then the mountain reflects that joy. It's not that I'm projecting it in an egocentric way, but my joy, my happiness, my tranquillity, and the mountain are in a mutual intercourse. I don't know what a mountain is by itself nor what I am by myself.

TRUNGPA RINPOCHE: You do admit that if you have a stomach upset, the mountain also has a stomach upset.

S: Yes, but I don't know what the mountain would be

or anything would be without there being that process of intercourse.

TR: That's not a problem. You're not going to lose your world if you don't have this definite intercourse. You don't have to extend your belly button into an umbilical cord. That was cut a long time ago, when you were born. It would be too complicated to renew your umbilical cord. Approaching things that way is part of the problem, in fact: if I have a world, is the world my prey? Or is it that the world is just the world and you're just you? There is a separateness that is in fact more of a grand union than anything else could be. Because of the separateness, there could be unity. Unity doesn't have to be glued together. In fact, that's what's known as imprisonment. You don't have to keep track of yourself particularly. You see the reflection of yourself anyway; the mountains are you anyway. If you get a headache, the mountains get a headache too, in your way of looking at them.

S: So there's no need to emphasize the belly button connection.

TR: That's right, that's right. If the mountains have a headache, just let it be that way.

STUDENT: How do you stop yourself from giving the mountains an aspirin?

TRUNGPA RINPOCHE: Is there any problem? Well, I'm not saying that you should feel pain and that therefore you should torture yourself. You can take an aspirin and, if you're severely sick, you can go to the emergency room at the hospital. There's no problem. I don't see any problems. We are not talking about starting a revolt against the world, guerrilla warfare against the rest of the world. We are talking about how to look at how to be with it, and I don't see any particular problems. You take aspirin, which is also sick at the same time. Because you are sick, your aspirin is sick as well. And then you take it, and because misery loves company, aspirin cures your headache.

STUDENT: Could you talk about the vipashyana experience in terms of the analogy of the tree we were using before?

TRUNGPA RINPOCHE: We are beginning to work on the level of minding the tree's business. We are at the point of picking up a pair of secateurs and beginning to crop the foliage leaf by leaf. This is the point we're at, but we haven't gotten into the details yet.

STUDENT: You've talked about panoramic awareness mostly in terms of awareness of environment. What I'm wondering is whether the vipashyana mode of operation would alter one's way of experiencing one's own thoughts or one's experience of, for example, the dream state. Would that be altered at the level of panoramic awareness?

TRUNGPA RINPOCHE: Those experiences are also your

environment. There is no environment other than your thoughts. Let's say you hit somebody, and this enemy of yours is approaching you again. You create a hostile environment, which is your thinking, your doing. If you get highly inspired by seeing some object associated with enlightenment, you create an environment of inspiration. Thoughts are your environment from that point of view, and there's no other environment besides that. You see, the whole thing is not really mysterious. It's always there and it's very literal and very obvious.

STUDENT: In meditation, I become aware of my theater performance, my lighting, my acting, and so on. Then I stop meditating and I'm back in the theater again.

TRUNGPA RINPOCHE: What's the problem?

S: Well, I thought there was some implication that from going and meditating and becoming aware of that theater, something would change. Or do I simply come back into the theater and be theatrical again?

TR: Well, not quite the same way. I think the real point is that we're talking about discipline. Actually, in a real theater group, in the Open Theater or other avant-garde theater groups, people feel they are disconnected from the theater world when they have to undergo some disciplined practice, which they usually call "warming up." The term "warming up" is a euphemism. In fact, warming up is a demand. There is the demand that before you turn on to performance, you warm up. The name deceives you, because while you are engaged in this discipline, you lose your theater.

S: Is theater going on here right now?

TR: Yes, but that's because you're not going through any particular training at this moment. You're just listening. It's very convenient and entertaining. But when you sit and meditate and you have an ache in your legs or a stiff neck, then the beautiful theater world begins to diminish.

STUDENT: May I say something? I'm enjoying this theater. This is a real experience for me, as real as meditation, and you're here doing theater, and I'm imagining that this is a real experience for you too.

TRUNGPA RINPOCHE: That's not enough.

S: What are we doing here, then?

TR: We're regrouping. At this point, we're regrouping rather than this alone being the goal. That is by no means true. What we're doing is not the goal. It's not the final product—as though you paid your money, got your ticket, and you're here watching, beautifully experiencing the final product. No.

S: It is part of the process.

TR: Part of the process, obviously.

S: Just as important as the discipline.

TR: Sure. But it's necessary to have the personal experience of facing yourself, which brings a reduction in your sense of showmanship. Meditation is the only way. Write that down.

STUDENT: Isn't what creates the theater the sense of one's own importance? If you think you're someone very important doing something very important, you have a tendency, as you say, to overwhelm the audience with your presence. But if you've got no sense of self-importance, or if you can manage to lessen your sense of self-importance, there's no theater. Who are you acting for? You're just here.

TRUNGPA RINPOCHE: I'm afraid it doesn't work as simply as that. Even if things are unimportant, you make theater out of the unimportantness. You always do that.

S: Why does theater always imply something contrived, not spontaneous, rehearsed?

TR: It does, because there's a sense of self-consciousness and a sense that you are the center of the game.

S: That's because you think you're important.

TR: Not necessarily. You might think you are terribly unimportant, but you can still sit on your toilet seat. And make yourself the center of the universe.

S: Why would you want to do that?

TR: That's it! That's it! That's the big question. We have to find out by sitting and meditating. That's the only way.

S: Well, I think—

TR: You can be told why you're doing so-and-so, but then you create further theater in relation to having been told that, you see?

S: You mean everything we do is theater.

TR: Yes, except meditating.

S: Why isn't meditating doing theater?

TR: If you meditate long enough, you find out that it's not so pleasant.

S: Doing theater isn't so pleasant either.

TR: It gives something.

S: It's horrible.

TR: It gives you some sense of survival.

S: You've got a sense of survival anyhow. You're here, you're surviving. I don't understand where the theatrics come in.

TR: They come in. That was a very theatrical remark you made.

S: If you say so.

TR: I do say so.

S: Okay. Now tell me why I don't exist. I have this belief that I exist. It's very real. And when you tell me that I don't exist, I get upset and frightened, and it really gives me a stomachache.

TR: That's it, that's it.

S: What's it?

TR: You are very threatened, right?

S: Very threatened. It's a terribly threatening idea.

TR: That's right. If you really did exist, you wouldn't feel threatened.

S: I'm threatened because you're supposed to know something that I don't know. And if you state that we don't exist, then, who knows, maybe you're right.

TR: Well, that's it.

S: You're the one that knows. As far as I'm concerned, I exist.

TR: Not necessarily. There are some possibilities that you don't. Look, that you came here, took the trouble to come here, is an expression of your nonexistence. Your listening to my crap and getting upset and threatened is an expression of your nonexistence.

S: Because I don't understand it. It's very hard to understand.

TR: That's right. There's nobody to understand, therefore you can't understand.

S: Well, it's very scary to think you don't exist. Then what the hell is going on?

TR: Good luck, madam.

S: I have good luck.

TR: With my compliments.

S: Thank you.

STUDENT: In *abhidharma* studies and other writings, it seems to be indicated that the point of shamatha practice is to develop *jhana* states. Without those, the literature seems to say, it is impossible to go on to the analytical processes involved in vipashyana. But you always caution us not to get involved in the concentration or absorption that leads to the jhana states, but to start out with mindfulness and go straight into panoramic awareness. Are these two different approaches that will both work, or will we have to get into jhana states eventually?

TRUNGPA RINPOCHE: If I may be so bold as to say so, this approach is superior to the one that encourages jhana states. If you become involved with jhana states, you are still looking for reassurance—the reassurance that you can experience the bliss of the jhana states—before you get into precision. I present it this way partly because that is the way I learned it myself from my teachers. My teachers trusted me. They thought I was an intelligent person, a smart kid, and that I could handle myself all right if they presented the teaching that way.

That is the same way I feel about relating with North American audiences. Every one of you people have done some kind of homework or other, though for the most part very painfully. You have some sort of ground that makes it possible to communicate things very freely to you, in the same way I was taught myself. So I have enormous trust in the audience at this point. People can grasp the point of view behind the basic training being given to them, so there is no need to reassure them through the experience of jhana states.

Jhana states are pleasurable states in which they could feel something definite and therefore conclude that the spiritual path really does exist, that everything is true after all. That approach is not necessary. You don't need the proof, which is a waste of time. Everybody is here, and they have already proved to themselves, maybe negatively, what's wrong with life, and they are looking for what might be right with it. In that sense, people have done their homework already, so they don't need further proof.

Jhana states are part of what is called the common path, which is shared by both Buddhists and Hindus. The application is that if somebody wants to get into a religious trip, theistic or nontheistic, they could be reassured through the jhana states that the religious trip does give you something definite to experience right at the beginning. It's a kind of insurance policy, which we do not particularly need. I think we are more educated than that. Nobody here is a stupid peasant. Everybody is a somewhat intelligent person. Every one of you knows how to sign your name. So we are approaching things with some sophistication.

S: So as one proceeds on the path through the yanas, and gets into the tantric yogas and everything, there is still no need to work on the jhana states?

TR: From the vipashyana level onward, it's no longer the common path, it's the uncommon path. You are getting into enlightenment territory rather than god-head territory. So jhana states are unnecessary.

They are similar in a way to what people in this country have gone through in taking LSD. Through that they began to realize that their life has something subtler to it than they expected. They felt that something is happening underneath. People took LSD and they felt very special. They felt there is something behind all this, something subtler than this. This is exactly the same thing that jhana states provide—the understanding that life isn't all that cheap, that it has subtleties. But in order to get into the vajrayana, you don't just keep taking LSD, which is obsolete from that point of view. That was just an opener, and you were exposed to a different way of seeing your life. You saw it from a different angle than you usually do. So in a way, taking LSD could be said to bring about an instant jhana state. In a way, it's much neater. Maybe LSD pills should be called jhana pills.

STUDENT: I'm interested in the point where you are self-conscious in the mindfulness of shamatha and then you switch into becoming panoramically aware. Does that switch happen in flips, in flashes? How does it work?

TRUNGPA RINPOCHE: What are you trying to find out, really?

S: I'm trying to classify my experience more, so I know when it's shamatha and when it's vipashyana.

TR: I don't see any problems there. When you experience shamatha, it's very literal, very direct, concise and precise. When you experience vipashyana, things begin to expand. Your mindfulness becomes more grown-up. You have a multifaceted awareness taking place, everything all at once. That is possible. It works. It has been done in the past, and we are doing it now. It's very simple. It's just like switching on a light switch—there's no problem, particularly.

But there are side effects, obviously. You start thinking, "What is this about to be? What should happen now?" and all kinds of things like that, which is unnecessary garbage. As far as that's concerned, when you meditate every day, it's like shaving every day. You shave off unnecessary little pieces of hair by meditating. So shave every day.

# 4

# *Boredom—Full or Empty?*

One of the points of basic vipashyana practice is developing what is known as the knowledge of egolessness. That is to say that the awareness that develops through the vipashyana experience brings nonexistence of yourself. And because you develop an understanding of the nonexistence of yourself, therefore you are freer to relate with the phenomenal world—the climate, atmosphere, or environment we have been talking about.

Unless there is no basic center, one cannot develop the vipashyana experience. On the practical level, this means that vipashyana is experiencing a sense of the environment, a sense of space, as the meditator practices. This is called awareness as opposed to mindfulness. Mindfulness is very detailed and very direct, but awareness is something panoramic, open. Even in following the breathing techniques of mindfulness of breathing, you are aware not only of the breathing but also of the environment you have created around the breath.

As far as dealing with heavy-handed thoughts, emotions, is concerned, there is no way of destroying or getting over them unless you see the reference point that is with them. To begin with, seeing this takes the form of awareness of the atmosphere or environment. If you are already aware of the atmosphere beforehand, then there is a possibility that you might have a less intense relationship with your heavy-handed thoughts. That is one of the basic points.

Once you are aware of the atmosphere, you begin to realize that thoughts are no big deal. Thoughts can just be allowed to diffuse into the atmosphere. This kind of atmosphere that we are talking about is, in any case, an ongoing experience that happens to us in our lives. But sometimes we find we are so wrapped up in our little game, our little manipulation, that we miss the totality. That is why it is necessary for students to begin with shamatha—so that they can see the details of such an eruption, such a manipulation, the details of the game that goes on. Then beyond that, having established some kind of relationship with that already, they begin to see the basic totality.

Thus vipashyana is understanding the whole thing. You might ask, "What is this 'whole thing'?" Well, it's not particularly anything, really. This "whole thing" is the accommodator of all the activities that are taking place. It is the basic accommodation, which usually comes in the form of boredom, as far as the practitioner is concerned. The practitioner is looking for something to fill the gap, particularly in the sitting practice of vipashyana meditation, where the quality of nonhappening becomes very boring. Then you might get agitated by the boredom, which is the way of filling it up with some activities.

So in this case, the background is boredom. There are different types of boredom that we usually experience. Insecurity, lack of excitement, being idle, nothing happening. In this case, in vipashyana, the boredom we are talking about is a sense of being idle, and this is unconditional boredom. The experience of vipashyana awareness has a quality of all-pervasive thick cream. It has body, at the same time it is fluid, and it is somewhat challenging. Therefore, as one's development of awareness is taking place, one doesn't become spaced out particularly, not at all.

When we talk about being spaced out, we are talking about being empty-hearted. When we are empty-hearted, then the dazzling light of emotions begins to irritate us. We can't grasp anything and we are ready to completely freak out. Whereas the vipashyana awareness is something much more tangible, in some sense, than this empty-heartedness. It is something very personal that exists. It usually accompanies any kind of activity, not only in sitting practice alone.

For example, sitting and listening to this talk, you have developed or created a certain type of attitude. You are directing your attention toward the speaker;

but also you know at the same time that you and the speaker are not the only people in this tent, so there is the sense that you are sitting in the middle of the inside of this space—underneath the ocean, so to speak. And awareness brings about your relating with that particular experience, which is tangible, real, experiential.

When awareness relates to that type of experience, it is called insight. Sometimes this is spoken of in terms of light, luminosity. But this doesn't mean something fluorescent. It refers to the sense of clarity that exists in this experience. Once you feel that basic all-pervasiveness, then there is nothing else but *that* (the other), and *this* (oneself) is long forgotten.

Maybe at the beginning *this* tried to struggle, to fight with *that,* the all-pervasiveness. But though *this* might struggle, at some point the all-pervasiveness is all over the place, and a sense of suffocation begins to develop. And that subtle suffocation turns into boredom. That is the point when you are actually getting into the all-pervasiveness of the vipashyana experience.

This is just the beginning stage of vipashyana that we have been describing. And I would like to emphasize once more that we are not talking about hypothetical possibilities. You can actually experience this in your life, in your being. And in fact, potentialities of vipashyana are already prominent in our experience; they take place all the time. But we have not actually acknowledged them or perhaps even seen them.

STUDENT: There are experiences in meditation where a certain openness takes place. But this openness seems to be different from boredom. It seems to punctuate the boredom. It is more exciting. It seems to be the opposite of boredom.

TRUNGPA RINPOCHE: At the introductory level, when you first have such experiences, obviously you feel excited. You feel that this is something new you've gotten. But as you use such experiences as part of your practice, you wear out the novelty of them very quickly—particularly in this case—and it all turns into a very powerful boredom.

When you are in a sauna, you like it at the beginning, and you like the idea, the implication, of being in a sauna. You like the sense of cleaning up and loosening up your muscles, and so on. But if you are stuck there, if somebody put a lock on your sauna-bath door, then you would begin to feel the heavy-handedness of it. You would get bored and frightened at the same time.

STUDENT: You spoke of suffocation turning into boredom and boredom then moving into some kind of openness. It sounds to me as though boredom is in fact a gut response to the fear of losing oneself, or losing selfhood. Is that the correct way of seeing it?

TRUNGPA RINPOCHE: I see it that way too, yes. The boredom is the atmosphere. While you are bored, you are not aware of *this,* but you're aware of the atmosphere, which creates boredom. That is a very interesting twist that takes place there, which doesn't usually happen in your ordinary life.

S: Instead of being afraid that the self is disappearing directly, you turn that outward, toward the situation.

TR: That's right, yes. That's the awareness experience that happens. Well said, sir.

STUDENT: When you're meditating and all of a sudden there's a sound in the room, like somebody coughs, sometimes you feel so susceptible to it that you feel very shattered. It's very magnified, very physical, electric. Is that an example of openness?

TRUNGPA RINPOCHE: There's something faintly suspicious there. It is possible that you become open and susceptible. But if you don't have a sense of the atmosphere as filled with body, with texture, then you are spacing out rather than connecting with shamatha or vipashyana. There is a definite need for you to deal with the, so to speak, dense, humid atmosphere.

STUDENT: How does being aware of the body and texture of the atmosphere, as you just said we should be, differ from being aware of the theater backdrop?

TRUNGPA RINPOCHE: That's the same thing, actually. In the theater you see not only the stage alone, but you have already created your own texture around the theater hall, and that thing, the stage, is more or less a highlight. If it weren't for that atmosphere, you wouldn't bother going to the theater. You'd watch television instead, or a movie. There's a difference between watching a movie and going to the theater. The movie has been produced already, and you are seeing the result. The play in the theater is being performed on the spot. Maybe the actors have their own stories, but still you are taking part in the performance somehow. Something might go wrong. Somebody might fall off the stage and break his neck. Whereas you can't expect that in the movies. All that is part of the texture of the atmosphere.

STUDENT: Is the kind of boredom that develops in vipashyana a different kind of boredom from the irritating boredom you have when you first start sitting?

TRUNGPA RINPOCHE: Well, I think it is a mixture of both. There are different kinds of boredom, obviously. The boredom that develops from irritation still has a reference point of *this,* whereas the boredom of boredom that develops in vipashyana is more all-pervasive, like having the flu.

S: So this involves more willingness to go all the way with the boredom.

TR: Well, that's the idea.

STUDENT: I thought of the boredom that occurred in meditation as being a problem of relating with emptiness, a problem of not being able to relate to the space because the space is empty. But you seem to be saying now that the boredom arises because you're relating to a space that is full, full of some kind of atmosphere.

TRUNGPA RINPOCHE: Those two amount to the same thing, actually.

S: I wonder how that is. There's the sense of boredom because the space is full, like when you've got the flu. In some sense it seems to me there that your environment is full of you.

TR: Which *is* emptiness.

S: How so?

TR: You see, when we talk about emptiness, we are not talking about a vacancy.

S: Is this emptiness in the sense of meaninglessness or—

TR: No, not even that. We are talking about emptiness as having a body or texture of emptiness, which is the same as saying it's full.

S: Well, does it have to do with the accommodation aspect? Is that what you mean by emptiness here, that there is something to hold the atmosphere?

TR: It's not the accommodation alone, but accommodation as well as the container that's containing.

S: You mean like the edges, the container itself that holds whatever's in it?

TR: Yes, which becomes the same thing as what's in it. For example, if you have a cup full of water, that is the epitome of emptiness. In fact, it's indestructible emptiness.

S: Indestructible because whether it has water in it or not, there's a space there?

TR: No. There's water already; you can't change that. Whereas if it's vacant, then you can fill it up with something else.

S: So acknowledging the water would be like acknowledging space.

TR: I don't think so. It's acknowledging the existence of the cup filled with water rather than any of those partial aspects. If you get involved with the aspects, then you have a problem. The boundary between them becomes problematic. If you acknowledge what is inside as nothing, then the boundary becomes troublesome. The boundary begins to haunt you.

S: So it's a sense of acknowledging the whole thing.

TR: Yes. That's what vipashyana is all about.

STUDENT: I wish you would be a little more specific about the boundary you were talking about. What were you referring to? Is it some sense of the limit of your horizon in the environment? Or is that your self-consciousness?

TRUNGPA RINPOCHE: It's the idea that you can get away from the boredom. You feel that there is this thing there, and you can deal with it.

S: So this is the beginning stage of vipashyana, and making the boundary would be like the stronghold of ego—

TR: Yes.

S: Still trying to—

TR: Still trying to escape, yes.

S: Trying to contain it somehow?

TR: Yes. Like thinking that if you know the blueprint for meditation, then you can get away from it. You know what's supposed to happen to you, so you can tune yourself that way in advance so you don't have to go through too much trouble.

STUDENT: Would a possible trick of the same sort be to just name your experience or go back to something you know, like a more shamatha-like approach? Just to try and get on top of your experience?

TRUNGPA RINPOCHE: Yes. Anything you can think of. Thinking about the hassles of life is another one. There are limitless outs.

STUDENT: Does that mean that a further vipashyana experience would be the breaking of the cup, breaking of the boundaries?

TRUNGPA RINPOCHE: The cup doesn't have to break. It dissolves. There is no warfare, particularly. The cup becomes water.

STUDENT: In that case, using the word *emptiness* seems to be very misleading. The opposite word would be even better: fullness.

TRUNGPA RINPOCHE: Fullness means security to a lot

of people. You know, for example, hunger is opposed to fullness. So *emptiness* may be the best word to express fullness.

STUDENT: You spoke of neurosis and you mentioned it in relation to self-existing suicide. I'm wondering whether everything, all neurosis, a person's whole being, doesn't always get back to the basic question of one's existence.

TRUNGPA RINPOCHE: Very much so.

S: Everything I do or think is trying to establish an answer to that question.

TR: Yes, definitely.

S: And is neurosis the ego confusing itself to death?

TR: It doesn't quite die. It prolongs the pain and gives birth to further pain. That's the terrifying part of it. Really stopping yourself completely, right down to nothing, wouldn't be very easy. Somehow, even after suicide, you still have to make sure that you are dead. And then a further attempt to make sure you are dead comes on. So your suicide never ends. That's the tricky part.

# 5

# From Raw Eggs
# to Stepping-Stones

In connection with awareness, there is something we should understand about the relationship between open mind and discipline, maybe a difference between the two or maybe a cooperation between the two. In talking about open mind, we are referring to a kind of openness that is related with letting self-existing awareness come to us. And awareness is not something that needs to be manufactured: when there is a gap, awareness enters into us. So awareness does not require a certain particular effort. Such an effort is unnecessary in this case.

Awareness is like a wind. If you open your doors and windows, it is bound to come in.

As far as discipline is concerned, sometimes we have problems or hesitation in relation to the experience of awareness not being desirable. We feel somewhat uncomfortable about being in the state of awareness. It makes us unable to indulge in the usual neurosis, which is seemingly more pleasurable—or at least it occupies our time. But a state of awareness somewhat creates a sense of alienation: we are unable to keep going with our ego's hang-ups and with our ego itself. Therefore, there is often a natural repulsion of the potential of enlightened mind or of enlightened mind itself.

This kind of discomfort always follows a state of awareness, and in many cases it could become quite exaggerated. You deliberately try to cast off that potentiality of enlightenment and a certain sense of fear connected with it that you don't want to get into. You might call this effort being conscious of yourself or being religious or whatever terminology you might come up with. But the whole thing boils down to this particular hesitation—you don't want to get into the state of awareness.

There is a definite psychological blockage here with a well-known case history, so to speak. There is a desire for the neurosis and less desire for the sanity. However, all the same, when we have been completely eaten up by insanity or neurosis, tremendously hassled by it, a superficial desire does arise to make a long journey to find basic sanity, a desire to seek out a teacher and read books about the spiritual path. But then, when we begin to do it, to put the teachings into practice, the same resistance is still there. It always occurs; it is a common psychological hang-up.

For example, there is the naughty schoolboy mentality. You try to find all kinds of excuses so you won't have to sit and meditate. You constantly cook up excuses to evade the practice. "I have to tie my shoelaces. Let's take some time on that. I know eventually I have to go sit and meditate, but let's just take a little time." Or, "I have to make a quick phone call." All these kinds of little hesitations have their root in a neurosis of a particular type that doesn't want to give in to the possible state of awareness. That is the natural situation concerning obstacles to openness.

Discipline cuts through that—but not by regarding it as a big problem or a big hang-up. It just simply uses the resistance as a stepping-stone. From there you walk into the state of awareness. That way the resistance becomes more of a help or a reminder than an obstacle. This is a question of a real, direct attitude.

Openness and awareness, as I have explained many times before, is a state of not manufacturing anything else; it is just being. And there is a misunderstanding, particularly in connection with vipashyana, which regards attaining awareness as an enormous effort—as if you were trying to become a certain unusual and special species of animal. You think: now you're known as a meditator, so now you should proceed in a certain special way, and that way you will become a full-fledged meditator. That is the wrong attitude. One doesn't try to hold oneself in the state of meditation, the state of awareness. One doesn't try painfully to stick to it.

If we take the term in a positive and creative sense, we could say that awareness is a state of absent-mindedness. The point here is that when there is no mind to be absent, energy comes in, and so you are accurate, you are precise, you are mindful—but absent-minded at the same time. So maybe we can use the term *absent-minded* in this more positive sense, rather than the conventional sense of being forgetful or constantly spaced out, so to speak. So whenever there is a message of awareness, then you are in it already. There is the state of absent-mindedness and mindfulness at the same time.

Absent-mindedness in this case acts as the instigator or evoker of the background, and mindfulness is the occupant of that background. So you are there, but at the same time you are not there. And at the same time you can fulfill your daily duties, relate to your living situation, your relationships, carry on conversations, and so forth. All that can be handled mindfully as long as there is absent-mindedness as the background. Which is very important.

Approached in this way, mindfulness is no longer a problem, a hassle, or a big deal. For that matter, it is not energy-consuming at all. This is a matter of taking a different slant in your attitude. The first step is that you are willing to be mindful. You have to commit yourself. In some sense, you have to take a kind of vow that you are willing to be mindful and aware. This is like saying to yourself: "This is my work for today and for the rest of my life. I'm willing to be aware, I'm willing to be mindful." When you have such a strong and real conviction to begin with, there are no further problems at all. Any further problems are just some kind of frivolity, which tries to overrule your memory that you should be mindful. So once you have taken that attitude of commitment, that commitment automatically brings absent-mindedness, which then results in your being mindful constantly.

So it's a question of commitment, which is also known as discipline.

You might ask, "What kind of commitment are we talking about? Am I supposed to sign on the dotted line? Am I supposed to join the club?" For the most part, neither of those approaches work. Once you join a club, that's it. Your name is on the membership list and the mailing list, and they do the job for you. You really have nothing to do. If you feel bored, you come to the club and you do their little things—ceremonies, dinner parties, celebrations, whatever they have. And you feel nice that you have your private club. You might receive a certificate with the name of the club, or a certificate with your special title done in calligraphy and with seals or whatever they have. That's nice to have around the house, but it doesn't really do anything for you. It's just a piece of paper. It was another ceremony that took place in your life. It's gone, it's empty.

So if it's not this join-the-club approach, what kind of commitment are we talking about in this case? It is actual commitment that requires constantly living in a special way. And what is that special way of living? It's just a memory that is a living memory rather than a past memory: the memory that you took a vow that you were going to be an aware person, that you were going to develop awareness throughout your life. That memory. And when you have that memory, it's not dead. It's really a living memory; it's a situation in your life. Having that kind of memory is a present situation, an up-to-date situation. Because of that memory, absent-mindedness occurs, and from that absent-mindedness, mindfulness develops. That is the basic instruction for how to handle mindfulness.

There are a lot of misunderstandings about this issue. People often feel that they have to be specially aware of what they are doing, and they walk that way and they sit that way. They behave as if they had a raw egg on their head. Consequently their life becomes lifeless, rigid like a dead body, and so solemn, so "meaningful." And there's no enlightenment in it; it 's all dead. Of course, there is some faithfulness in it, and some kind of joy or pride, but somehow even the presence of those don't serve to cheer those people up. This has been a problem in the way people work with awareness.

When we talk about the process of developing mindfulness and awareness, we are talking about practicing a living tradition, not renewing an old culture, a dead culture. This is a living tradition that has been practiced for twenty-five hundred years by millions of people. It's always up to date, and we can practice it the same way as those who came before us. It is a very personal experience, so personal that it is actually workable.

So that seems to be the basic idea of how to conduct one's basic awareness program, so to speak.

STUDENT: I'm very interested in the distinction you made between ordinary absent-mindedness and this special absent-mindedness. I seem to have a great deal of ordinary absent-mindedness, and I was wondering if there was energy in that that could be transformed into the kind that provides the right background for mindfulness.

TRUNGPA RINPOCHE: Forgetfulness is not being absent-minded in the true sense. In that case, you are so much involved in your own world that you lose loose ends constantly. In the true absent-mindedness we talked about, your mind is gone, properly and completely, without anything to occupy it. And I think the only way to shift from one kind of absent-mindedness to the other is the kind of vow we discussed. With that vow, you are making a definite step, a definite effort toward something else. You are already self-involved and forgetful, and this is a step toward something else. It's not particularly a matter of solving the problem of our old-fashioned absent-mindedness by replacing it with a new one, but it's a definite jump. You need some kind of commitment in your life that says, "Now I'm going to do this." That should bring some kind of psychological change. Without that, you can't change, because your habit pattern just goes on and on.

S: It sounds as though the ordinary absent-mindedness is the opposite of the new kind. It's turned inward on itself, whereas the new kind is more opened outward.

TR: I think so too, yes. Well, I think some sort of personal influence is needed—an influence that moves you from one kind of message to another kind of message. If somebody tells you that if you eat a carrot you're going to die tomorrow, that gives you a shock. Then you take a vow: "From today onward, I will never eat a carrot." And then, whenever you think of a carrot, you think of that, and whenever you think of that, you think of a carrot.

S: I'll try not to eat carrots.

TR: That's not the point. Anyway, help yourself.

STUDENT: This commitment you're talking about sounds like something conscious you would do, but it doesn't seem that it could be conscious. It seems like it is something evolutionary. And if it is evolutionary, you can't do it. So how does one make that kind of commitment? How does one approach it?

TRUNGPA RINPOCHE: I'm afraid this is very primitive, nothing very subtle. Because we have constantly been deceived by our subtleties. This is a very ordinary, rugged commitment, very low-class maybe, if you want to put it that way. "From now onward, I'm going to do this." It's very conscious. But then you don't hang on to that. Once you've made the commitment, then you have that commitment there, transplanted into your mind already, and it begins to grow. So you have to have that primitive quality at the beginning. Otherwise, there's no kindling wood to light the big logs. It's very primitive and very literal, and perhaps very sudden as a highlight in your life. But obviously the effects that it has will not be very sudden. Obviously the effects happen slowly. You are not suddenly reformed in one second, but you have the potentiality of being reformed from then onward.

It's like having a birthday party. You don't suddenly go from twenty-one to twenty-two when you blow out the candles. Obviously not. You are becoming twenty-two as much earlier on as later, when your birthday celebration takes place. But all the same, you have to have some kind of landmark. Otherwise, we are too sneaky, and there's no other way of dealing with that.

STUDENT: It's like quitting smoking. You have to keep reaffirming your decision, but at one point, you have to say, "I'm going to quit smoking."

TRUNGPA RINPOCHE: I think it's different from quitting smoking. That is giving up something, which has a lot of problems involved in it. In this case, you are taking on something new, which is something more positive than just being starved to death.

STUDENT: You talked about using all those little tricks that we have for resisting meditation as a stepping-stone. Say you notice yourself doing this number—you're five minutes late and you're still tying your shoes, or whatever—you're aware of it and you just keep on doing it. So how does it become a stepping-stone?

TRUNGPA RINPOCHE: Use the resistance as the starting point of your practice. Now you have the resistance and you are going to use the resistance as part of your meditation. You're already meditating. You have awareness while you're trying to delay, you have the wind of meditation already in you. You can't even undo it. You're already plugged in.

# 6

## *Loneliness*

—◆—

I think we should realize that the practice of meditation takes us on a journey that is very personal and very lonely. Only the individual meditator knows what he or she is doing, and it is a very lonely journey. However, if one were doing it alone without any reference to the lineage,[8] without any reference to the teacher and the teachings, it would not be lonely, because you would have a sense of being involved in the process of developing the self-made man. So you would feel less lonely. You would feel like you were on the way to becoming a hero. It is particularly because of the commitment that one makes to the teachings and the lineage and the teacher that the meditative journey becomes such a lonely one.

That commitment does not particularly bring protection or companionship or feedback to clear away your doubts or resolve your loneliness. In some way your sense of loneliness is exaggerated by your commitment to the path. The path has been established and you start to take a journey on it. That journey is then up to you. You can read the map, which tells you how far along you are. You can stop at various places for rest and refreshment. But still it's your journey.

Even if you are sharing the journey with other people, those other individuals' experience is different, totally different, in terms of how the journey really affects them. So it's a lonely journey. There is no support, no specific guideline. You may have been told to do this and do that, but that is just at the beginning—so that you know how to be lonely.

So loneliness is one of the basic points. It means not having any security on this path of meditation. One can't even say that you get moral support. For one thing, as we discussed earlier on, you don't exist; and because of that, security doesn't exist. The only thing that is visible, that apparently exists, is the journey, the loneliness itself. That is a very important point for us to see and realize.

On this path, we are not looking for the grace of God or any other kind of saving grace. There is no sense that we are going to be saved, that someone is going to keep an eye on us so that if we are just about to make a mistake, someone will fish us out. If we had that sense, the journey would become a very sloppy one, because we could afford to play around. We would think that in case we did the wrong thing, we could be fished out or saved. But instead of relying on outside help, in this case, the impetus has to be a very personal impetus. Nobody is going to save us and nobody is going to protect us, so this journey has to be a very personal, individual journey. That's a very important point.

Now, the next question is the role of the teacher, the guru. How is he or she going to affect this process? There is no contradiction whatsoever between being on a lonely, personal journey and relating to a teacher. The role of the teacher is to teach the students what direction to take, to teach you a certain attitude and how that attitude might develop further. And the role of the teacher is to show you that the path is lonely.

In order to hear the clear message from the teacher without any misunderstanding, you have to have a sense of commitment and openness toward the teacher, who in this case is known as a "spiritual friend." He is not regarded as a learned professor, a mad scientist, or a magician, for that matter. Rather, the teacher is a friend who has conviction and enough openness toward himself or herself. Because of that, the teacher can be blunt and direct in pointing out the disciplines of the path. So to hear the clear message from the teacher, you have to have a sense of openness and surrender.

But this does not mean worshiping or adoring the teacher. You just need a sense of basic openness, a feeling that the teacher's approach to the teaching is accurate. The idea is not that it *has to be* accurate, but it happens to be accurate because of a certain relationship of commitment that evolves between you and your teacher. Because of that, the teacher's words become real to you; it's not like listening to a tale or a myth. What the teacher has to say becomes relevant to you.

That is what's called the meeting of two minds. What you experience and what the teacher has to say make sense together. A definite link of understanding develops. Though the dharma may be only partially understood, it still makes sense, it still becomes some kind of truth.

Your teacher has to be someone who lives on this earth at this very time. One shouldn't kick around such ideas as: "I have a heavenly teacher who tells me when I'm in trouble, sends me messages in my dreams, in my fantasies, and in my daydreams. I get these messages flickering through my subconscious jingle bell. The teacher is always there when I need him because he is a heavenly teacher, a celestial teacher." Ideas like this are quite deceptive. You always hear what you want to hear. Nothing is told to you about maybe some things needing correction. And certainly that heavenly teacher wouldn't talk about loneliness and aloneness. He wouldn't give you the teachings of aloneness and loneliness, because that heavenly teacher is a production of your mind. So for that reason it is necessary to have as a teacher a person who lives on earth, who is your contemporary, who shares the same world with you, the world of human beings. It is necessary to make a relationship with such a teacher in the sense of developing an understanding of each other.

Then there is another notion, which is the *sangha,* the community of practitioners working together. The sangha is also the creation of the teacher and the teaching in a sense. You get information, messages, from being among friends who are also doing the same practice as you at the same time. You might feel that you can take off by yourself whenever you want, that you can maintain yourself without having to be hassled by the sangha, without going through the painful problems of dealing with the rest of the community, these friends around you. But this is partially not accepting the world of the teachings. You want just to have a summit meeting with your teacher and to try to avoid the rest of the flock. You go off in order to be saved from the hassle of relating with anybody else. This is also in part looking for something other than loneliness—looking for security. Although your style of dealing with the whole thing is the style of loneliness, actually dealing with the sangha would make you feel more lonely. And that is very painful.

The sangha carries the atmosphere of the teacher and the teaching and the lineage. Sharing that experience together makes more sense. Relating with the teacher becomes also relating with the community, the sangha. But although this process is very necessary, it should not be regarded as a source of security. The idea is not that if you feel strange and odd, you feel better if you see someone else strange and odd. The idea is not "Misery loves company." The idea is not that because there are a hundred or a thousand or a million people doing the same thing as you, you feel secure because you're not the odd man out. The idea is more that you are the odd man out in any case, and there are lots of odd men out together. You don't confirm each other's paranoia or shyness or sense of insecurity, but the sangha helps—in the long run or even in the immediate situation. For example, if you want to chicken out of your sitting practice and you are in the midst of seventy or a hundred people sitting together, when you are about to get up to walk out, you feel somewhat strange, uncertain. And that kind of very simple and literal encouragement to practice is necessary.

People often have a certain kind of attitude toward the others: "I am above them. I have special credentials, a special intelligence. I don't want to be completely associated with the mass, the flock. When I feel bored or lonely, I would like to chat with them and be nice to them. They're interesting people to talk to. But when I feel really edgy and needy, the sangha freaks me out, so I should avoid them. I should have a summit meeting with my guru in his den." That attitude is problematic. Avoiding pain, avoiding loneliness is a problem. A lot of problems come from avoiding the sense of loneliness, of aloneness, from avoiding the sense of losing the ground of ego.

So it is necessary to have a spiritual friend who can work with you. And also around you and your spiritual friend, there are other, so to speak, lesser spiritual friends who are known as the sangha. They do not take on the role of instructors, but they do assume the role of friends—who are sometimes not particularly over-whelmingly friendly. Or at other times they may be rather kind. But that kind of relationship is necessary.

The whole point is that we have grown up with a very strange relationship to society. Sometimes we like society and are trying to get into it and become a rep-lica of everybody else. You do exactly the same thing as everybody else, and it feels good. You have a social standard to relate to and you have your M.A. or Ph.D. You are a professional person and you have a car of your own. You know how to cook food, entertain friends, and you are humorous and engaging. You are even eloquent and interesting. You are a good host, a good driver, an acceptable person, a nice guy.

But at the same time, you don't want to be like that at all. Your complex about society takes all kinds of forms. Sometimes you want to be above society and bring society up to your level. You are part of an exclu-sive lodge or club. Only highly evolved people can work with you, deal with you. You are not like the rest of the world, not like the others. You are special, very special. You eat different food. You even drive differently, maybe. You break the law in a different way—with conscious effort. You cook meals specially, and you talk a special way; you articulate differently. You put the accent on the metaphysical or mystical, or on being zany. Society pushes people into this kind of attitude because there are so many repetitions taking place.

On the other hand, sometimes people have the feeling that they can't even make it up to the repetitions level. They feel belittled, uneducated. But then, once you've gotten to that level and you feel you are just like everybody else, you want to rise above this and try to do special things. You acquire special art treasures, which you show. You develop a special handicraft or a talent that you have that is out of the ordinary. The selling point in all this is that it is very special, unlike anything else, that you are a very special person, which is another kind of neurosis that goes on in society. First you try very hard to be ordinary, and then, when you achieve that, you try to rise above the ordinariness.

There are all kinds of different levels and different approaches to trying to ignore the loneliness.

If you are like the ordinary person in the street, working a nine-to-five job, you feel very lonely. And also you felt very lonely before you got to the ordinary level. You felt you had to struggle, that you were wretched, outside of society. And then, when you try to step above the ordinariness into extraordinariness, you also feel lonely. All those attempts are made out of loneliness. The whole time the goal is not to be lonely, to achieve enormous security. So there are constantly inspirations arising out of the sense of loneliness. But at the same time, the loneliness is always rejected. You are always trying to achieve the opposite of loneliness, always looking for companionship. That seems to be the problem.

So we have two kinds of processes here. Rejecting loneliness by using the medium of loneliness; and trying to use the medium of friendship and companionship to arrive at the goal of loneliness. The second one is the dharma way. At the beginning you have your spiritual friend and your sangha that you work together with. It feels good, fantastic. But once you have been initiated into the path and style and practice of meditation, then your goal is loneliness. You begin to realize that.

Loneliness here is not meant in the sense of feeling alone in an empty room with nothing but a mattress. When we talk about loneliness here, we are talking about the fundamental starvation of ego. There are no tricks you can play; there is no one you can talk to to make yourself feel better. There's nothing more you can do about the loneliness at all. So for that reason, there's a need for a teacher, for the sangha, and a need for practice.

This is not based on a theistic approach—needing

protection, needing a savior. As far as that is concerned, everybody is their own savior. The basic point is that the practice of meditation brings all kinds of experiences of uncertainty, discontentment of all kinds. But those experiences seem to be absolutely necessary. In fact, they seem to be the sign that you are on the path at last. So we can't do publicity by having testimonials for meditation practice. If we did, it would be disastrous.

But this has been pointed out many times in the books and the teachings. It has been said over and over that this journey is not particularly pleasant; you have to shed your ego. And still at the beginning there is a certain fascination about it. You start to think, "I wonder what it'd be like without ego. That's another point of view. Let's try it. It might be exciting. After all, we've tried all the other things." Such inquisitiveness is necessary. We have to start at a very primitive level. At the beginning, inquisitiveness of this kind is absolutely needed. We think, "I wonder what it would be like to have a spiritual friend. It seems it's quite exciting. I'm going to go up to Vermont to see the guru. I'm going to pack my bag and go. It's so exciting." But then we are here and the truth of the matter begins to dawn on us. When we get back, people might ask us, "What did you get out of that? Did you learn anything? Are you enlightened now?"

Well, . . . perhaps we should have our discussion.

STUDENT: It seems that meditation is a means for us to recognize habits and deal with them. Is that correct?

TRUNGPA RINPOCHE: What do you mean by "deal with"?

S: Acknowledge them.

TR: Yes, that's right.

S: Is our entire samsaric mind just habits?

TR: Habits cannot exist without a reference point, the reference point being duality: if that [anything] exists, then I exist; if I exist, then that exists. That's where the basic split begins to happen.

S: Can you describe how shamatha and vipashyana relate to habit?

TR: Habit comes from habit. You are told how to do meditation, and then you develop some new habits. But some new style develops, obviously, and those new habits are not so habit-oriented. In fact, it's very difficult to make meditation into a habit. Even though you've been doing it for twenty years, still there's constantly a certain sense of struggle involved. This shows that meditation is different from the rest of habitual things. It requires some kind of challenge, constantly.

STUDENT: The loneliness you've described is really nothing more than the root of the tree you were talking about earlier, except viewed from a slightly different perspective, right?

TRUNGPA RINPOCHE: What do you mean by "nothing more than"?

S: Nothing really is, and so nothing can really be more, can it?

TR: That's right, yes.

S: So loneliness and the root of the tree are describing the same thing.

TR: Yes. I think as you go along, the rug is pulled out from under your feet. So there are different stages of that.

S: But the thing that occurred to me that is kind of cute is that there's no condition under which the root of the tree isn't, which means that everything is the path. Okay?

TR: Yes.

S: If the root of the tree equals loneliness and loneliness equals the path, then you can't really fall off, right?

TR: That's right. And you see, that then gives the understanding that once you are on the path, you can't shake it off, so to speak. It becomes part of you, all the time, whether you like it or not. Once you begin to join in, you can't undo it, because you can't undo your basic being.

S: Thank you.

TR: So there's no need to look for security.

S: It's not there. I mean, there's no security anyway.

TR: It's not there, right. That's right. That's a good one.

STUDENT: My connection with the word *loneliness* has to do with different emotional states like sadness and all that sort of thing. It seems that you're talking about something different, but if so, I don't understand it.

TRUNGPA RINPOCHE: Maybe it is an emotional state of some kind, but not in the sense of the highlight when your emotion reaches its peak. Rather, it's a self-existing situation. Whenever there is uncertainty and threat, there is loneliness, which is the fear of no companionship and the fear that nobody understands you—which is very simple. At the same time, it's a fear that you might possibly not exist, that there's nothing to work on, nothing to work with. We might even go so far as to say that it's a sense of total nonexistence or total deprivation. A feeling that whatever direction you face, you're facing the world rather than the path. Things are being pushed back on you. It's some subtle state of wretchedness. I mean, it's a heavy one. It's a very total wretchedness, all-pervasive. It's not just one-directional, such as, "Because he treated me badly, therefore I feel lonelier, and I'm sobbing." It's not just him alone, but it's the whole orchestra that is not playing your music.

STUDENT: To go back to the idea of not being able to fall off the path, it seems to me—and you've written this too—that it is possible to get sidetracked. Even more so the further along you are on the path. So in a sense you can fall off the path, even for a long time.

TRUNGPA RINPOCHE: You could, I think, if you are

distracted unconsciously, without the help of meditative awareness. On the other hand, if you are very deliberately, very consciously trying to give up the path, you can't. Therefore, there is a need for constant awareness practice. It's a way of checking, so to speak. Not checking up for the purposes of security, but just to be there. And if you get fed up with that and decide to give it up, you can't do it. But it's true, you can get caught by sidetracks that come as a product of unawareness. That's why, you know, everything has been thought out about the path. That's why meditation is prescribed, why mindfulness and awareness are prescribed. So awareness is a way to keep straight on the path.

S: So you keep coming back to your original practice.

TR: Yes, but not in order to be a good boy or anything like that. Just to be yourself properly.

STUDENT: I'd like to ask a question about loneliness and love. In my experience, the kind of love where two people try to be together in order to protect themselves from loneliness hasn't worked out too well. When you come in contact with the loneliness, it seems to destroy a lot of things you try to pull off in trying to build up security. But can there be love between two people while they continue to try to work with the loneliness?

TRUNGPA RINPOCHE: That's an interesting question. I don't think anybody can fall in love unless they feel lonely. People can't fall in love unless they know they are lonely and are separate individuals. If by some strange misunderstanding, you think you are the other person already, then there's no one for you to fall in love with. It doesn't work that way. The whole idea of union is that of two being together. One and one together make union. If there's just one, you can't call that union. Zero is not union, one is not union, but two is union. So I think in love it is the desolateness that inspires the warmth. The more you feel a sense of desolation, the more warmth you feel at the same time. You can't feel the warmth of a house unless it's cold outside. The colder it is outside, the cozier it is at home.

S: What would be the difference between the relationship between lovers and the general relationship you have with the sangha as a whole, which is a whole bunch of people feeling desolateness to different degrees?

TR: The two people have a similarity in their type of loneliness. One particular person reminds another more of his or her own loneliness. You feel that your partner, in seeing you, feels more lonely. Whereas with the sangha, it's more a matter of equal shares. There's all-pervasive loneliness, ubiquitous loneliness, happening all over the place.

STUDENT: Would you say that loneliness is love?
TRUNGPA RINPOCHE: I think we could say that.

STUDENT: You've indicated that as we got into this loneliness, there would be a lot of wretchedness as well. Now I'm wondering how compassion fits into this picture. How does one practice compassion with that loneliness?

TRUNGPA RINPOCHE: I think loneliness brings a sense of compassion automatically. According to the Buddhist scriptures, compassion consists of *shunyata*, nothingness, and knowledge, *prajna*. So that means the ingredients of compassion are the experience of non-ego and a sense of precision, which is often also called skillful means. You can't have compassion unless you have egolessness and the sense of precision at the same time. The sense of egolessness, obviously, comes with loneliness. And the sense of precision is seeing the wretchedness and at the same time seeing through oneself, so that everything's been examined and looked at. That becomes compassion. That's unconditional love, unconditional loneliness. Then even after you've reached that point, the loneliness principle goes on. But then you are not lonely anymore; it becomes aloneness as opposed to loneliness, which brings a sense of space.

STUDENT: You have talked a lot about boredom in meditation. You even said somewhere that if you were not bored, you were stupid, or like a cow. And now you've just said that even after twenty years, meditation would always be a challenge. I'm having trouble following what you mean by boredom. Is the boredom a kind of touch-and-go thing where sometimes you're bored and when you're bored it causes you to act; and then you act for a while and get bored again? Or are you talking about a continual boredom?

TRUNGPA RINPOCHE: We are talking about a continual boredom.

S: Then what about the challenge that keeps coming up?

TR: Boredom has different textures. Sometimes it's a challenge, but it's just a challenge rather than anything extraordinary. It's not a challenge in the sense of having a vision or a mystical experience in which an actual demon comes and tries to attack you. We are not talking about those kinds of challenges. We are talking about a very ordinary challenge, a very boring challenge. But still you have to do something about it. It's like if you swallow a bug in your soup. It's a challenge afterward. But it's not extraordinary that there's a bug in your soup. You've known bugs for a long time. You've known soup for a long time. Those are very boring things. But the combination of the two makes interesting boredom.

S: Maybe it's the word *boredom* itself I don't understand. Is that interesting boredom the same as, for example, if you're working on a building or a piece of sculpture every day for six months, every morning there's something—there's a bug. But if you look at it from a larger perspective, it's just the same boring challenge every day.

TR: Yes, yes.

S: So in other words, at the same nine-to-five job, you could either get fat and stupid, or you could look around.

TR: I think so. I mean we can't carve something extraordinary out of boredom. And we'd better not do that.

S: So then the problem is perhaps just not seeing that as boredom. Which means that you're not looking.

TR: That's right. Yes.

STUDENT: You're recommending that everyone should find a teacher for themselves who they could have a relationship with. How do you go about identifying a person who could be a good teacher?

TRUNGPA RINPOCHE: Finding a good teacher is not like buying a good horse. It's a question of relationship. If the teacher actually speaks in your style, connects with your approach, if what he says has some bearing on your own state of mind, if he understands your type of mentality, then he is a worthwhile teacher. If you can't understand what the teacher has to say, that's a lot of hassle at the beginning. Then, after he's said it, you have to try to interpret, and there's a lot of room for misunderstanding. So there should be a sense of the teacher's clarity and some kind of link between you and that teacher. The type of mentality and the type of style have to be synchronized.

S: But also the teacher has to have something else. I mean, you could have good communication with a member of the sangha, maybe, but you're both in the same boat. Whereas the teacher has to have something more to give.

TR: Yes, the teacher has to be a leader in some sense. Otherwise, he couldn't keep up with the sangha. The sangha would get to be over the teacher's head. The teacher would go down and down. Obviously, yes. But at the same time the teacher should be a traveler too, someone who is traveling with you. That's very important. Rather than being stuck with enlightenment and unable to go beyond it.

STUDENT: Back on the question of loneliness, are you saying that one sees one's loneliness in someone else? And if you're saying that, does that lead to the conclusion that one can never find release from loneliness in being with anyone else?

TRUNGPA RINPOCHE: That's right. And loneliness can stretch as high as to enlightenment, which is a greater loneliness. Hopeless, eh?

S: Just a drag.

TR: Maybe a transcendental drag, actually.

# 7

# Creating a Little Gap

———

Unfortunately, for lack of time, we haven't had a chance to go into the subject of vipashyana in great detail. But I think you must have some idea of the approach that should be taken. At this moment, I would like to place further emphasis on the idea of postmeditation awareness. That seems to be the heart of Buddhist meditation practice, along with the actual sitting practice.

If you have any sense of openness to the practice of meditation, the important point is to commit yourself to the practice. This brings a sense of reality, that the practice is no longer a myth. It's a real experience. And having become a part of your lifestyle, the practice could be utilized as a reminder, a way of taking a look at your heavy-handed thoughts, which are known as emotions. A complete new world, an old new world, of meditative life could be established.

There is so much joy that goes with that. This is not frivolous joy, but a sense of being connected with the earth. Finally, you are no longer kidding anybody, including yourself. There is something here that is very basic, that is founded on very solid ground. There is real discipline taking place, and you don't have to depend on hocus-pocus anymore as comic relief or a way to cheer up. I think that this particular experience could be said to be the beginning of basic sanity, which begins to dawn on us. Now your life contains discipline, and discipline reminds you of awareness, and awareness also reminds you of discipline. So an ongoing process is developed.

With the help of a teacher, with the help of fellow sangha members, and with the help of the examples of lineage holders, life becomes a very full one—completely full but at the same time very spacious.

The basic notion there is that once you have developed a sense of awareness, a glimpse of awareness, that glimpse of awareness cuts through the karmic chain reactions that reproduce karmic debts, because it creates a little gap that sets chaos to the karmic chain reactions' productivity. So the karmic chain reactions are cut, and that slows down further reproduction of ego-centered karma. So the basic logic is that awareness practice is the way we can stop or transmute samsara.

One can't stop samsara immediately, because samsara is at the same time the inspiration for freedom. Without samsaric experience, we are unable to reach this level of working toward freedom, and because of samsara's hang-ups, we are able to do so. So there is no particular regret about samsara.

Still we have to realize that the practice of awareness does not represent the ultimate hope or the ultimate salvation in the evangelical sense. But it is real, and a very honest and earnest step we are taking in committing ourselves to the practice of meditation. It's not particularly colorful. It's something that everybody on the spiritual path does, and everybody does it relatively accurately. Otherwise they wouldn't be on the spiritual path. At the same time, it contains a lot of sophistication. A lot of training toward prajna, or transcendental knowledge, takes place through it. An educational process takes place. We begin to learn how to look at things, how to look everywhere, anywhere, with a certain reference point that is other than the reference point of duality. We are able to see things very clearly, very precisely, and maybe there is a tinge of joy—which is not necessarily an extraordinarily happy one. It's not particularly pleasurable, but there is a sense of joy, a sense of lightness, and at the same time a sense of fullness that takes place constantly.

Having said too much about that, I think perhaps we should have a short discussion, and then we should close our seminar.

STUDENT: All through this seminar you've been talking about boredom. Now you talk about joy. Can one experience boredom and joy together?

TRUNGPA RINPOCHE: Making friends with the boredom is the joy. We are not talking about two different subjects or trying to run the hot tap and then the cold tap and put the two together into some great happy medium. We are saying that boredom *is* openness and joy is also openness.

STUDENT: Yesterday we were talking about love and relationships. In terms of Buddhism, what is the validity of having a relationship with one person if falling in love just comes from loneliness? Is the validity of such a relationship just another illusion?

TRUNGPA RINPOCHE: Well, illusion is not supposed to be looked down upon. In any case, everything's illusion, so you can't say this is *just* an illusion, therefore it does not have enough worth. When you have a very close personal relationship with a person such as your mate, your husband or wife, that person becomes the spokesman for the rest of the sangha. When you live with somebody long enough, there is intense irritation and intense warmth. Often you regard each other as being very cute and sweet, but sometimes as a living devil or devilette. There are a lot of unexplored areas of experience, and you only get to use your microscope with your own mate. With others there's no time to use it. Nobody else will sit there and let themselves be scrutinized and take the trouble to scrutinize you. Only your mate will put up with that, which is a very generous thing, fantastic. So in that way, your mate becomes a spokesman for the rest of the world. That seems to be a very important part of one's life. You can't just shake it off or take it lightly.

STUDENT: You talked a lot about a commitment to meditation, and I couldn't help connecting that with something I have heard of called the refuge vow, which I understand is part of the Buddhist tradition. Could you say something about that?

TRUNGPA RINPOCHE: Very simply, the idea of the refuge vow is becoming a Buddhist. This entails ignoring sidetracks. From the point of taking the vow onward, you take a straight and narrow path. You are no longer fascinated by sidetracks, so your shopping trip is over. You no longer shop around for something else.

Of course this is very much related to the practice of meditation. You might ask, "How is it possible to really connect with the practice of meditation? What positive move could I make to get into that situation?" It is making this commitment to give up shopping for something else. This is not like committing yourself to the church or the pope or the bishop. Rather, you make a commitment to yourself that you are going to work on yourself through the practice of meditation. That is actually necessary. And as I have already said, there is a need for a definite date, a definite occasion like a birthday celebration. You do need a certain time and space, so people can come and watch you taking the vow in a ceremony conducted by your preceptor. It is saying that from today onward, from this very hour on, you are going to be a meditator. That is the point.

In the long run, I think it is very important and necessary for people to do that. But in the short run, I wouldn't recommend to people just to jump in, not until they know what they are doing. They should have a self-existing commitment already evolved in themselves before they take such a vow—which is dangerous. Once you have done it, you are stuck there. You can't undo it. It is very claustrophobic, and no one can save you from it. You can't untake the refuge vow. That is unknown. But when a person is involved in working with himself or herself, then at that point, there is a need for taking the refuge vow. But taking the refuge vow is not like going on welfare and getting free service. You become a refugee, you become homeless. You don't have any home ground. You are stateless, you don't have a passport anymore. You're stuck with the area where you are. You have become a refugee and you can't travel around with your passport anymore. The basic point is cutting down speed and neurotic playfulness.

STUDENT: I thought being a refugee meant going to another country to take shelter.

TRUNGPA RINPOCHE: Not necessarily, not in this case. Here being a refugee means you lost your country.

S: So you take refuge in yourself?

TR: You take refuge in the Buddha as example, the dharma as path, and the sangha as companionship. In other words, you take refuge in how other refugees carried out their refugeeship.

S: And no land?

TR: No-man's-land. You don't have to pay tax.

STUDENT: How do you know if you're meditating correctly or not, apart from the fact that you get bored?

TRUNGPA RINPOCHE: I think you know that it's not particularly a metaphysical situation. It's a real situation. You have experience. There's a constant awareness continuing, rather than that you meditate in the verbal sense. But if you sit for two hours and you are only there twice for one second, then something must be wrong there. You can tell there's something wrong if the rest of the time you were completely gone. You are not there. It's very simple.

S: When you say you're gone, what's the difference between that and sitting there and your thoughts going other places?

TR: If you are aware of your thoughts, there's no problem. Whereas if you are fantasizing a complete journey, to the point of packing your suitcase, buying an airplane ticket, and flying off to India, if you work out what places to visit, what stuff to buy, what gurus to visit, then come back, arrive at the airport in your country, your people greet you at the airport, and then the meditation gong rings ending the session—then there's some problem there.

S: So the difference would maybe be that if you did that trip but came back and said, "Oh, I just did that trip," then that's meditating?

TR: Meditating here is a very definite thing—is being aware, meditating with what's happening. It's the developing-awareness thing we've been talking about for the past few days.

STUDENT: I heard you once said that being in nowness was not necessarily being aware of the present thoughts, the discursive thoughts, that that wasn't essentially being in nowness. In meditating, if you're aware of the discursive thoughts that are going on—

TRUNGPA RINPOCHE: That's just awareness.

S: But that's not necessarily being aware of nowness?

TR: No, which is impossible to do. So we do our best. Nowness-like is awareness.

Well, we have to close our seminar now. I would like to request you to continue to pay heed to what we have discussed and try to do something about it, do something about your meditation practice. A lot of you sat and practiced, and hopefully you will be able to continue that way, to give the practice a certain amount of time in your life. This will help you a great deal. And also then the time and energy that we put in here will not be wasted. Then this property of ours will not have served for the further reinforcement of karmic debts but as a cause to free people from their karma. So I hope you'll be able to work harder on your practice. Please, please, please do so. It is very important. It may seem that we have a lot of time to get around to things, but at the same time it is very urgent. Neurosis is constantly creeping in. A lot of people are being put into painful situations by that insanity. So we have a lot of responsibilities. You should consider relating to your friends, your parents, and your key people, whoever you are associated with. It's up to you whether you are going to relate to them in terms of bringing down a samsaric mess on them or trying to give some help. This doesn't mean to say that you should convert everybody to Buddhism. You have to behave yourself first. And in order to do that, you need to do lots of practice, lots of sitting meditation. There is a chain reaction that takes place. You personally hold a very important place in your universe. Thank you.

# Notes

1. The implication is that since the technique remains with the natural simplicity of what we are doing already anyway instead of being a clever or innovative departure, there is very little provocation for turning our meditation into a goal-oriented project. Even the attention to the breath, the most deliberate aspect of the technique, cannot be turned into a "big deal," since it is to receive only a light, 25 percent touch.

*Spiritual materialism* refers to the approach of trying to use spiritual techniques to achieve the goals of ego, such as becoming calmer, more efficient, more magnetic, or simply happier. This attitude toward spirituality, always widespread, was particularly rampant in the "spiritual supermarket" days of the 1970s, when these talks were given. A major feature of Trungpa Rinpoche's early teaching was a thoroughgoing critique of this attitude, and his first major book was called *Cutting Through Spiritual Materialism.* He sought to show that the true approach to meditation, and spirituality in general, was continuously surrendering the reference point of ego rather than finding ways to fortify it.

2. *Lhak-thong* literally means "superior seeing," which is taken to mean seeing clearly. It is the Tibetan term for the form of meditation, common to nearly all traditions of Buddhism, known as vipassana in Pali and vipashyana in Sanskrit. This is the principal subject of the second seminar in this book. Here Trungpa Rinpoche translates this term as "awareness." Usually, however, he translates this term as

"insight," and thus refers to vipashyana as "insight meditation." Nonetheless, he regularly refers to the primary experience of vipashyana practice as awareness, contrasting it with mindfulness, the focus of shamatha practice.

3. Mahayanists might prefer to argue from the principle of shunyata, nothingness, which teaches that all things are devoid of an essence. Thus the self, too, they would say, is devoid of an essence: there is no ego to which one can cling. But the direct experiential logic presented here is more suited to the simplicity of hinayana, and coincidentally very well represents the vajrayana approach to egolessness as well.

4. These are described in detail in Chögyam Trungpa, *The Heart of the Buddha* (Boston: Shambhala Publications, 1991), pp. 21–58.

5. One of Trungpa Rinpoche's frequent descriptions of the process that goes on in the first stages of meditation is "making friends with oneself." An account of this is found in Part Two of this book, chapter 2, "Recollecting the Present."

6. "Akashic records" is a semijocular allusion to a notion popularized by the Theosophical movement. Trungpa Rinpoche apparently makes use of this term, familiar to many people in his audience, in order to avoid at this point having to get into a technical explanation of his own.

The idea is that the record of one's good and bad deeds, one's karma, is kept in some transcendental realm (*akasha* is Sanskrit for "space") and continues to affect one throughout subsequent lifetimes. The Buddhist notion corresponding to some extent to this is the so-called "storehouse of consciousness" (Skt. *alaya vijnana*), where past actions leave imprints or memories. These karmic imprints produce a tendency in the future toward repetition of actions similar to the ones that produced them. The Buddhist notion, though fulfilling a roughly equivalent function, differs significantly from the Theosophical one. It is more impersonal, since in the Buddhist view, there is no definite ego or self that transmigrates from rebirth to rebirth. Also, there is no deity or other watcher who judges the karma good or bad, other than the specious watcher trumped up by ego.

7. Here Trungpa Rinpoche is once again referring to the clumsy and painful sense of me-ness connected with the basic split, duality.

8. The heart of the Buddhist tradition is a lineage of students and teachers who receive and transmit the awakened state of mind as a living experience from one generation to the next.

# *Glossary*

———

The definitions given in this glossary are particular to their usage in this book and should not be construed as the single or even most common meaning of a specific term. Unless otherwise designated, foreign terms in the glossary are Sanskrit.

*abhidharma*   The systematic and detailed analysis of mind, including both mental process and contents. Also, the third part of the Tripitaka, the "three baskets" of early Buddhist scripture.

*ati* (also *maha ati*; Tib. *dzogchen*)   "Great perfection." The ultimate teaching of the Nyingma school of Buddhism in Tibet. Ati is considered the final fruition of the vajrayana path. It is known as the great perfection because in its view the original purity of mind is always already present and needs only to be recognized.

*bhumi*   "Land." Each of the ten stages that the bodhisattva must go through to attain buddhahood: (1) very joyful, (2) stainless, (3) luminous, (4) radiant, (5) difficult to conquer, (6) face-to-face, (7) far-going, (8) immovable, (9) having good intellect, and (10) cloud of dharma.

*bodhisattva* "Enlightenment being." One who has committed himself or herself to the mahayana path of compassion and to the practice of the six paramitas, or transcendental virtues: generosity, discipline, patience, exertion, meditation, and knowledge. The bodhisattva takes a vow to postpone his or her own personal enlightenment in order to work for the benefit of all sentient beings.

*bodhisattva path* Another name for the mahayana.

*buddha* This term may refer to the principle of enlightenment or to any enlightened being, in particular to Shakyamuni Buddha, the historical Buddha.

*crazy wisdom* (Tib. *yeshe chölwa*) Primordial wisdom that radiates out spontaneously to whatever situation is present, fulfilling the four enlightened actions of pacifying, enriching, magnetizing, and destroying. Crazy wisdom goes completely beyond convention. Thus, though the crazy-wisdom person's behavior may appear mad or outrageous to others, he or she always automatically destroys whatever needs to be destroyed and nurtures whatever needs to be cared for.

*hinayana* The "lesser" vehicle, in which the practitioner concentrates on basic meditation practice and an understanding of basic Buddhist doctrines such as the four noble truths.

*jnana* The wisdom-activity of enlightenment, transcending all dualistic conceptualization.

*Kagyü* (Tib.) "Command lineage." One of the four principal schools of Tibetan Buddhism. The Kagyü lineage is known as the "Practice Lineage" because of its emphasis on meditative discipline.

*mahamudra* "Great symbol or seal." One of the highest meditative teachings of the vajrayana, transmitted especially by the Kagyü school. Inherent luminosity and precision of mind, which is both vivid and empty.

*mahayana* The "great vehicle," which emphasizes the emptiness (*shunyata*) of all phenomena, compassion, and the acknowledgment of universal buddha nature. The ideal figure of the mahayana is the bodhisattva; hence it is often referred to as the bodhisattva path.

*nidana* The twelve "links" that form the chain of conditioned arising: (1) ignorance, (2) formations or impulses, (3) consciousness, (4) name and form, (5) the six realms of the senses, (6) contact, (7) sensation, (8) craving, (9) clinging, (10) becoming, (11) birth, and (12) old age and death.

*paramita* "That which has reached the other shore." The six paramitas, or "perfections," are generosity, discipline, patience, exertion, meditation, and knowledge.

*prajna* "Transcendental knowledge." Prajna, the sixth paramita, is called transcendental because it sees through the veils of dualistic confusion.

*Rudra* In the Hindu tradition, Rudra was an aspect of the deity Shiva. In the Buddhist vajrayana, he is the personification of the destructive principle of ultimate ego. Tradition tells that he was a tantric disciple who perverted the teachings and eventually killed his guru. Rudrahood is the complete opposite of buddhahood.

*samadhi* A state of total meditation in which the mind rests without wavering and the content of the meditation and the meditator's mind become one.

*samsara* "Journeying." The vicious cycle of transmigratory existence. It arises out of ignorance and is characterized by suffering.

*shunyata*   "Emptiness." Complete openness, devoid of specific essence.

*tantra*   "Continuity." A synonym for vajrayana, the third of the three main yanas of Buddhism in Tibet. *Tantra* also refers to the root texts of the vajrayana.

*tathagata*   Literally "thus gone," an epithet for a fully realized buddha.

*vajrayana*   "Indestructible vehicle." The third of the three main yanas of the buddhadharma, the yana of fruition. In the vajrayana, buddhahood is presented as already actual through the skillful means of visualization, mantra, and mudra.

*yana*   "Vehicle." A coherent body of intellectual teachings and practical meditative methods related to a particular stage of a student's progress on the path of buddhadharma. The three main vehicles are the hinayana, mahayana, and vajrayana.

# Transliterations of Tibetan Terms

| | |
|---|---|
| drubgyü | *sgrub brgyud* |
| dzogchen | *rdzogs chen* |
| gewe she-nyen | *dge ba'i bshes gnyen* |
| lhakthong | *lhag mthong* |
| lhakthong dagme tokpe sherap | *lhag mthong bdag med rtogs pa'i shes rab* |
| shi-lhak sungjuk | *zhi lhag zung 'jug* |
| drenpa nyewar shakpa shi | *dran pa nye bar gzhag pa bzhi* |
| yeshe chölwa | *ye shes 'chol ba* |

# About the Author

---

VEN. CHÖGYAM TRUNGPA was born in the province of Kham in Eastern Tibet in 1940. When he was just thirteen months old, Chögyam Trungpa was recognized as a major *tülku,* or incarnate teacher. According to Tibetan tradition, an enlightened teacher is capable, based on his or her vow of compassion, of reincarnating in human form over a succession of generations. Before dying, such a teacher leaves a letter or other clues to the whereabouts of the next incarnation. Later, students and other realized teachers look through these clues and, based on careful examination of dreams and visions, conduct searches to discover and recognize the successor. Thus, particular lines of teaching are formed, in some cases extending over several centuries. Chögyam Trungpa was the eleventh in the teaching lineage known as the Trungpa Tülkus.

Once young tülkus are recognized, they enter a period of intensive training in the theory and practice of the Buddhist teachings. Trungpa Rinpoche (*Rinpoche* is an honorific title meaning "precious one"), after being enthroned as supreme abbot of Surmang monastery and governor of Surmang District, began a period of training that would last eighteen years, until his departure from Tibet in 1959. As a Kagyü tülku, his training was based on the systematic practice of meditation and on refined theoretical understanding of Buddhist philosophy. One of the four great lineages of Tibet, the Kagyü is known as the "Practice Lineage."

At the age of eight, Trungpa Rinpoche received ordination as a novice monk. After his ordination, he engaged in intensive study and practice of the traditional monastic disciplines as well as in the arts of calligraphy, thangka painting, and monastic dance. His primary teachers were Jamgön Kongtrül of Sechen and Khenpo Kangshar—leading teachers in the Nyingma and Kagyü lineages. In 1958, at the age of eighteen, Trungpa Rinpoche completed his studies, receiving the degrees of *kyorpön* (doctor of divinity) and *khenpo* (master of studies). He also received full monastic ordination.

The late fifties were a time of great upheaval in Tibet. As it became clear that the Chinese Communists intended to take over the country by force, many people, both monastic and lay, fled the country. Trungpa Rinpoche spent many harrowing months trekking over the Himalayas (described in his book *Born in Tibet*). After narrowly escaping capture by the Chinese, he at last reached India in 1959. While in India, Trungpa Rinpoche was appointed to serve as spiritual adviser to the Young Lamas Home School in Dalhousie, India. He served in this capacity from 1959 to 1963.

Trungpa Rinpoche's first opportunity to encounter

the West came when he received a Spaulding sponsorship to attend Oxford University. At Oxford he studied comparative religion, philosophy, and fine arts. He also studied Japanese flower arranging, receiving a degree from the Sogetsu School. While in England, Trungpa Rinpoche began to instruct Western students in the dharma (the teachings of the Buddha), and in 1968 he cofounded the Samye Ling Meditation Centre in Dumfriesshire, Scotland. During this period he also published his first two books, both in English: *Born in Tibet* and *Meditation in Action.*

In 1969, Trungpa Rinpoche traveled to Bhutan, where he entered into a solitary meditation retreat. This retreat marked a pivotal change in his approach to teaching. Immediately upon returning he became a lay person, putting aside his monastic robes and dressing in ordinary Western attire. He also married a young Englishwoman, and together they left Scotland and moved to North America. Many of his early students found these changes shocking and upsetting. However, he expressed a conviction that, in order to take root in the West, the dharma needed to be taught free from cultural trappings and religious fascination.

During the seventies America was in a period of political and cultural ferment. It was a time of fascination with the East. Trungpa Rinpoche criticized the materialistic and commercialized approach to spirituality he encountered, describing it as a "spiritual supermarket."

In his lectures, and in his books *Cutting Through Spiritual Materialism* and *The Myth of Freedom,* he pointed to the simplicity and directness of the practice of sitting meditation as the way to cut through such distortions of the spiritual journey.

During his seventeen years of teaching in North America, Trungpa Rinpoche developed a reputation as a dynamic and controversial teacher. Fluent in the English language, he was one of the first lamas who could speak to Western students directly, without the aid of a translator. Traveling extensively throughout North America and Europe, Trungpa Rinpoche gave hundreds of talks and seminars. He established major centers in Vermont, Colorado, and Nova Scotia, as well as many smaller meditation and study centers in cities throughout North America and Europe. Vajradhatu was formed in 1973 as the central administrative body of this network.

In 1974, Trungpa Rinpoche founded the Naropa Institute, which became the only accredited Buddhist-inspired university in North America. He lectured extensively at the Institute, and his book *Journey without Goal* is based on a course he taught there. In 1976, he established the Shambhala Training program, a series of weekend programs and seminars that provides instruction in meditation practice within a secular setting. His book *Shambhala: The Sacred Path of the Warrior* gives an overview of the Shambhala teachings.

In 1976, Trungpa Rinpoche appointed Ösel Tendzin (Thomas F. Rich) as his Vajra Regent, or dharma heir. Ösel Tendzin worked closely with Trungpa Rinpoche in the administration of Vajradhatu and Shambhala Training. He taught extensively from 1976 until his death in 1990 and is the author of *Buddha in the Palm of Your Hand.*

Trungpa Rinpoche was also active in the field of translation. Working with Francesca Fremantle, he rendered a new translation of *The Tibetan Book of the Dead,* which was published in 1975. Later he formed the Nalanda Translation Committee, in order to translate texts and liturgies for his own students as well as to make important texts available publicly.

In 1978 Trungpa Rinpoche conducted a ceremony empowering his son Ösel Rangdröl Mukpo as his successor in the Shambhala lineage. At that time he gave him the title of Sawang, or "earth lord."

Trungpa Rinpoche was also known for his interest in the arts and particularly for his insights into the relationship between contemplative discipline and the artistic process. His own art work included calligraphy, painting, flower arranging, poetry, playwriting, and environmental installations. In addition, at the Naropa Institute he created an educational atmosphere that attracted many leading artists and poets. The exploration of the creative process in light of contemplative training continues there as a provocative dialogue. Trungpa

Rinpoche also published two books of poetry: *Mudra* and *First Thought Best Thought.*

Trungpa Rinpoche's published books represent only a fraction of the rich legacy of his teachings. During his seventeen years of teaching in North America, he crafted the structures necessary to provide his students with thorough, systematic training in the dharma. From introductory talks and courses to advanced group retreat practices, these programs emphasize a balance of study and practice, of intellect and intuition. Students at all levels can pursue their interest in meditation and the Buddhist path through these many forms of training. Senior students of Trungpa Rinpoche continue to be involved in both teaching and meditation instruction in such programs. In addition to his extensive teachings in the Buddhist tradition, Trungpa Rinpoche also placed great emphasis on the Shambhala teachings, which stress the importance of mind-training, as distinct from religious practice; community involvement and the creation of an enlightened society; and appreciation of one's day-to-day life.

Trungpa Rinpoche passed away in 1987, at the age of forty-seven. He is survived by his wife, Diana, and five sons. His eldest son, the Sawang Ösel Rangdröl Mukpo, succeeds him as president and spiritual head of Vajradhatu. By the time of his death, Trungpa Rinpoche had become known as a pivotal figure in introducing dharma to the Western world. The joining of his great appreciation for Western culture and his deep understanding of his own tradition led to a revolutionary approach to teaching the dharma, in which the most ancient and profound teachings were presented in a thoroughly contemporary way. Trungpa Rinpoche was known for his fearless proclamation of the dharma: free from hesitation, true to the purity of the tradition, and utterly fresh. May these teachings take root and flourish for the benefit of all sentient beings.

# Meditation Center Information

For further information regarding meditation or inquiries about a dharma center near you, please contact one of the following centers.

Karmê-Chöling
Star Route
Barnet, VT 05821
(802) 633-2384

Rocky Mountain Dharma
Center
4921 County Road 68C
Red Feather Lakes, CO
80545
(303) 881-2184

Vajradhatu Europe
Zwetchenweg 23
D3550 Marburg
Germany
49 6421 34244

Vajradhatu International
1084 Tower Road
Halifax, N.S. B3H 2Y5
Canada
(902) 425-4275

Many talks and seminars are available in cassette tape format. For information, call or write:

Vajradhatu Recordings
1084 Tower Road
Halifax, N.S. B3H 2Y5
Canada
(902) 421-1550

For information about Buddhist postsecondary education, write or call:

The Naropa Institute
2130 Arapahoe Ave.
Boulder, CO 80302
(303) 444-0202

For information about a magazine published by students of Chögyam Trungpa, focusing on meditation and the contemplative arts, contact:

Shambhala Sun
P.O. Box 399, Halifax Central
Halifax, N.S. B3J 2P8
Canada
(902) 422-8404

# INDEX

# THE DHARMA OCEAN SERIES